SIMPLY STARS

QUILTS THAT SPARKLE

ALEX ANDERSON

"…a star danced, and under that I was born."

—William Shakespeare, 1616

C&T PUBLISHING

Simply Stars is designed not
only for the quiltmaker,
but also for those who are
interested in teaching it as a class.
A suggested class outline
follows the projects.

Simply Stars
Quilts that Sparkle
© 1996 Alex Anderson

Editor: Lee Jonsson
Technical Editor: Joyce Engels Lytle
Copy Editor: Judith M. Moretz
Cover and book design: Rose Sheifer Graphic Productions
Electronic illustrations: Rose Sheifer Graphic Productions
Photography: Sharon Risedorph
Author photo: Michael Stefanski

Attention Teachers:
C&T Publishing, Inc. encourages you to use this book
as a text for teaching. Contact us at 800-284-1114 or
www.ctpub.com for more information about the C&T Teachers Program.

Library of Congress Cataloging-in-Publication Data
Anderson, Alex   (Alexandra Sladky)
Simply stars : quilts that sparkle / Alex Anderson.
        p.   cm.
        Includes index.
        ISBN 1-57120-019-3 (pbk)
1. Patchwork—Patterns. 2. Quilting—Patterns. 3. Stars in art.
        I. Title
        TT835.A53 1996
746.46'041—dc20   96-15854

Published by C&T Publishing, Inc.
P.O. Box 1456
Lafayette, CA 94549

Heirloom is a registered trademark of Hobbs Bonded Fibers.
HG Television is a registered trademark of The E.W. Scripps Company.
Omnigrid is a registered trademark of Omnigrid Inc.
Pellon is a registered trademark of Freudenberg Nonwovens, Pellon Division.

Printed in China
10 9 8 7

TABLE OF CONTENTS

DEDICATION

To John, Joey, and Adair,
You are the brightest stars in my life. May your love and kindness
continue to shine through all your lifelong journeys.
Love, Alex (Mom)

ACKNOWLEDGMENTS

To all my students, you have been my best teachers!
To "Strings," my minigroup, for all the support and love you've given
me throughout the years; Susanne M. Rasmussen, for your expedience
and excellent machine quilting; Joyce Lytle and Lee Jonsson, for
helping me make my dream a reality; Jennifer Sampou, for your inspirational designs; and C&T Publishing, for believing in me.

INTRODUCTION

Twinkle, twinkle, little star,
How I wonder what you are,
Up above the world so high,
Like a diamond in the sky,
Twinkle, twinkle, little star.

—Jane Taylor, 1824

How many stars can there be in the universe? For centuries scientists have admired and studied stars. Poets and writers have tried to capture their essence in a single line or two. Many children have wished upon the first evening star, while women and men can even boast drifting through space among them. Throughout time people have loved and celebrated stars. Stars remind us of the vastness of our universe and of what is possible if we learn to reach for our stars.

As quiltmakers we continue to carry out this celebration of stars in our quilts. Whether they are the primary component or a subtle surprise, stars appeal to both the traditional and innovative quiltmaker. As my friend Bernice McCoy Stone would say, "They have stood the test of time." We never tire of looking at or playing with stars.

What is learned from star making affects all other avenues of quiltmaking. *Simply Stars* teaches you how to make stunning star quilts by applying foolproof techniques to exciting fabric combinations. With just a few simple guidelines you will achieve dynamic results.

When I started teaching stars, my star class focused primarily on the technical (piecing) aspects of star making. But as the class began to develop, it took on a life of its own (just as our quilts do)! I found students were willing to experiment with unusual and exciting fabric combinations, making each successive star more elaborate and interesting than the one before. Every star block became an opportunity to try different color and fabric possibilities. Even simple stars in delightful colors and fabrics produced dramatic quilts.

As your interest in star quilts grows, you will find the number of star patterns endless. In an effort to provide a solid base of understanding, *Simply Stars* is designed to examine stars composed of four basic shapes: squares, rectangles, triangles, and diamonds. With the information covered in this book you will learn techniques that carry over into many different areas of quiltmaking, and are paramount to successful quiltmaking regardless of the patterns used. Following are the types of stars included in the book.

- ♦ Stars Made of Squares and Triangles
- ♦ Stars Made of an Isosceles Triangle in a Square
- ♦ Stars Made of Diamonds and Y Seams

Each star shape is represented with several different six inch and twelve inch blocks along with twelve specific quilt projects. Each block and project is complete with cutting numbers (or patterns) and piecing instructions. I recommend you begin your star journey in the beginning of this book, as the stars are presented in order of difficulty.

As a celebration of students' work, the Star Gallery explores many creative avenues of star making and quilt design. For their quilts the students combined many of the traditional stars presented in the twelve different quilt projects included in this book. Note how the students combined interesting fabric and design elements in their star quilts. I thank my friends for generously sharing their work with us.

Be prepared for an inspirational adventure into star making. This journey will take you in wonderful new directions. May all your precious stars shine bright!

Magic (Cutting) Numbers

The star quilts in this book are based on four basic shapes: squares, rectangles, triangles, and diamonds. These quilts already include magic (cutting) numbers used for rotary cutting. You will find rotary cutting saves times and is extremely accurate.

If you want to change the size of the block, use the magic (cutting) numbers. These numbers remain constant no matter what size block you are making. There are two basic rules for using the magic (cutting) numbers.

1. The magic (cutting) numbers given will only work with a ¼" seam allowance.

2. Measure the finished size of the desired piece and add the magic number to that size. Do not take into consideration the ¼" seam allowance; the magic number does that for you.

SQUARES AND RECTANGLES

Measure the finished size of the desired piece and add ½".

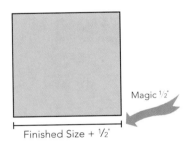

Magic ½"

Finished Size + ½"

TRIANGLES

Triangles can be a little tricky. First you must decide if you want a half-square triangle or a quarter-square triangle.

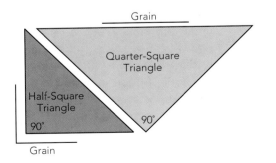

The difference between the two triangles is where the straight of the grain ends up. The half-square triangle has the two sides adjacent to the 90°

corner on the straight of grain. The quarter-square triangle has one side opposite the 90° angle on the straight of grain. You always want the outside edge of the pieced unit or block to remain on the straight of grain. (If not, your block will stretch and become unusable).

Half-Square Triangle

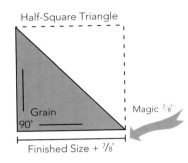

Half-Square Triangle

Grain

90°

Magic ⅞"

Finished Size + ⅞"

Cut a square the finished size plus ⅞", then cut ◹.

Quarter-Square Triangle

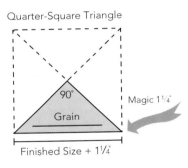

Quarter-Square Triangle

90°

Grain

Magic 1¼"

Finished Size + 1¼"

Cut a square the finished size plus 1¼", then cut ◻.

Isosceles Triangle in a Square

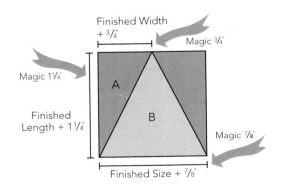

Finished Width + ³/₄"

Magic ¾"

Magic 1¼"

A

B

Finished Length + 1¼"

Magic ⅞"

Finished Size + ⅞"

The isosceles triangle in a square is a simple shape to cut. Keep in mind that the star tip has a left and a right, much like a vest or blouse. You must always cut the star tips in double layers, keeping like sides together. This will give you a left and a right. (This is my method, but there are other reliable methods that use templates or rotary cutting techniques.)

A: STAR TIP

Cut one strip the finished width plus ¾". Then fold lengthwise and cut a rectangle the finished length plus 1¼". Cut the rectangle corner to corner. This will give you two left and two right star tips.

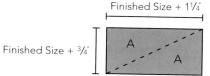

B: BACKGROUND

Cut a square the finished size plus ⅞", then cut as shown.

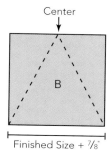

If all your B triangles are from the same fabric, cut a strip the finished size plus ⅞", then cut as shown.

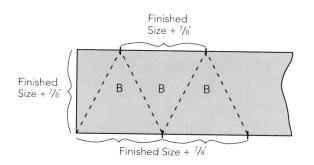

45° DIAMONDS

When working with a diamond, measure the distance between the parallel lines and add ½". This is unlike the previous measurements we have taken where we measured the edge of the shape.

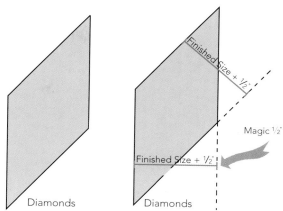

To achieve the 45° cut, use a ruler with a 45° line marked. I recommend the Omnigrid® rulers, especially the 6" x 12" ruler.

Cut the strip the appropriate width. Then position the strip and ruler as shown.

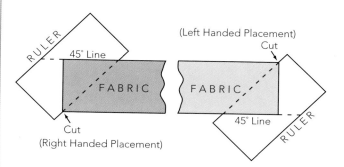

Cut the initial 45° cut. Slide your ruler across the cut strip to the appropriate measurement, keeping the 45° line on the edge of the strip. Remember you are measuring the width between the parallel lines.

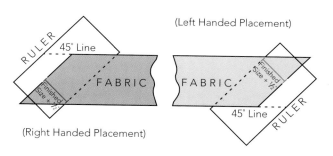

Note: If the diamond is elongated, the pieced diamond unit will have a left and a right side. Cut a strip the finished width plus ½" by the full width of fabric. Fold the strip lengthwise and cut 45°. Move the ruler and make the second cut.

GENERAL INSTRUCTIONS

Yardage

As a self-proclaimed fabric lover I find it restricting to work with a set amount of fabric. After deciding on the look of my quilt I like to incorporate as many different fabrics as possible. Therefore, as you approach each project in this book, keep in mind the fabric amounts listed are the smallest amounts you will want to purchase. Even though fabric stores cut a quarter yard minimum, you still want to purchase a wide variety of fabrics for your quilt, or look through your existing stash (your support system) for added variety.

Prewashing

As an ardent fabric collector I manage to mooch fabric from the most unusual places. Not knowing all my fabrics' histories, I think it is prudent to at least test for color-fastness and shrinkage. I usually do this in my washing machine, using warm water and mild detergent, and checking for water with a strange tint. All quilters have their own philosophy on this subject; however, I can assure you it is a sad day when your new, crisp, white masterpiece has turned a dull shade of pink. It can weaken the heart of even the strongest quiltmaker!

Cutting

The cutting numbers given for each project are for one block. If you want to cut more than one block, stack, press, and cut up to four layers. To ensure accuracy, never cut more than four layers at once.

Simple Hints for Perfect Stars

The following discussion on points, pinning, and pressing (also known as the technical stuff) is especially useful for making stars.

Points

The success of a perfect star rests not only on a dynamite fabric selection, but also on getting the points perfectly placed. How disappointing when you have spent time and money choosing a great fabric set, mastered rotary cutting, and then your star tips get cut off. You want the tips on each block to float one-quarter inch in from the unfinished edge and the angles to align exactly on the seams. If you take just a few precautions your stars will look great.

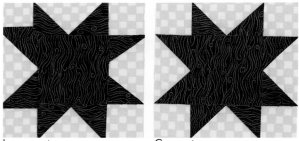

Incorrect   Correct

ALL-STAR LINEUP

The challenge with star making is working with several different shapes that often appear not to fit together. If your cutting has been handled correctly, it's just a matter of learning how the shapes fit together. The All-Star Lineup gives you a pictorial guide of how to align odd shapes that will be sewn together.

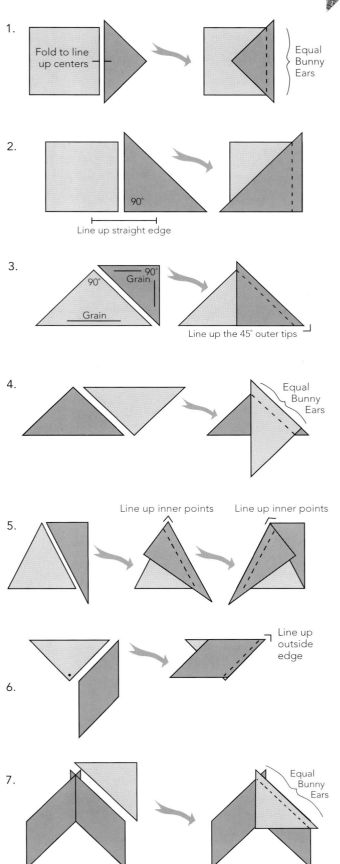

1.

Fold to line up centers

Equal Bunny Ears

2.

90°

Line up straight edge

3.

90° 90°
Grain
Grain

Line up the 45° outer tips

4.

Equal Bunny Ears

5.

Line up inner points   Line up inner points

6.

Line up outside edge

7.

Equal Bunny Ears

After you have pieced your shapes together and are confident you have resolved their pairing successfully, it's time to trim off the bunny ears. If something looks off, do not trim. With the "ears" still intact, you can remeasure to make sure the initial cut was correct.

Once you have assembled the individual units which when combined will complete your star, it is time to sew them together. I find it helpful to lay out the block before assembling the units.

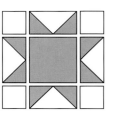

Look carefully where the tips intersect. It is important they occur one-quarter inch in from the unfinished edge.

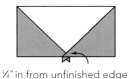

¼" in from unfinished edge

When sewing the units together, if one of the sections has a one-quarter inch intersection, always place it on top. You want to see where the intersection is occurring. Sew one hair to the right-hand side of the intersection. This allows for pressing. If the intersection has to be on the bottom, and you cannot see it, mark the point with a pin.

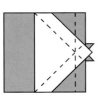

SEAM RIPPING

On occasion you will have to pick out a seam. Here are a few simple guidelines to keep in mind.

1. Use a seam ripper with a small, sharp tip.

2. Set your stitch length just long enough so your seam ripper slides nicely under each stitch.

3. If the two units are each sewn on the bias, consider throwing out the piece and starting over. The chance of stretching the units is almost 100 percent.

4. Pick out every third stitch on one side, then lift the thread off on the other side. Never pull and stretch the fabric.

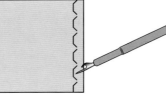

Keeping these rules in mind will make seam ripping easier and less problematic when re-sewing.

Pinning

To pin, or not to pin: that is the question. People generally have very strong opinions about this issue and are often not willing to change. I have found the little time it takes to pin can determine the success of the block! (I guess you know what camp I'm in.) Basically, you should pin where there are seams and intersections that need to line up. Here are some further guidelines to successful pinning.

1. Use glass head, extra-sharp, fine pins. They are costly, but worth every penny. Fat, dull pins will shift the alignments.

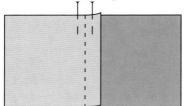

2. When aligning seams, drop a pin in both sides of the seam no more than ⅛" from each side.

3. If you have two components that need to align exactly, drop the first pin in from the wrong side of A (exactly at the intersection), inserting into the right side of B (exactly into the intersection).

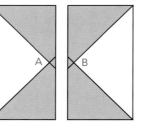

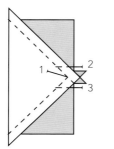

Press the head of the pin firmly into both intersections. While holding the pin tautly in place, place second and third pins on each side of the intersection, no more than ⅛" out. Let first pin dangle loosely.

As you approach the intersection, remove the first pin at the last minute, letting your sewing machine needle drop into the same hole. I have found this technique works ninety-eight percent of the time!

Pressing

Last, but not least, you must evaluate your pressing techniques. Quilters have varied approaches to pressing, and this alone can determine the success of your star! Here are a few simple guidelines that are as important as your fabric selection:

1. Press on a firm surface.

2. Pre-press your fabric before you cut into it. If the fabric seems to lack body or feel limp, spray starch it and press. It is important the fabrics all feel the same in weight. Pre-spraying with starch or sizing will help achieve this. Then proceed to cut into it.

3. Once you have cut the shapes, *never* press the unit until it is necessary to direct the seams. This can inadvertently stretch any exposed bias.

4. When pressing (moving) the seams to one side or the other, approach the pieced unit with the iron from the straight of grain edge. Avoid touching any exposed bias with the iron.

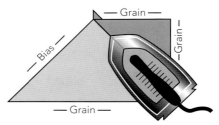

5. Press on the right side of the fabric (unless the seams are being pressed open). This will help avoid pressing tucks into the seams.

6. In this book, press in the direction the arrows indicate. The seams are pressed in certain directions for ease of construction, not pressed from light fabric to dark.

7. When six or more seams come together, consider pressing the seam open. This will help the star lie flat. These rules might seem a little rigid and perhaps overwhelming; however, they are great habits to develop. So many variables come into play when star making; it is best to avoid obvious problem areas where you have some control. You will come to appreciate the time and agony these tips will save you.

Fabric

Fabric, fabric, fabric! In quiltmaking it is the biggest decision we have to make. For many people it is a paralyzing experience. I prefer to look at it as an opportunity to expand my understanding of color. I once had a teacher in college who stopped me in my tracks when I was complaining about the use of different colors. She said, "To say you hate a color tells me you are ignorant of its use." Needless to say, that was a life-changing experience for me. Now I treat every bolt of fabric in every color family as a potential candidate.

First you must decide on the theme or look of your quilt. This decision rests on the fabric you use. This can become a delightful journey if you open your mind and use fabrics that might not be your first choice. My rule of thumb is, the more fabric you can incorporate into your quilt, the more exciting it will be (true confessions of a fabric lover). The important thing is to decide on a theme and run with it. Fabric is the soul of your quilt. Even the simplest block can sing with exciting fabric combinations. Here are a few ideas to get your mind moving. Create and have fun! Remember, the possibilities are endless.

Holiday

This is a safe way to start, and the results are always stunning. When we think of different holidays, certain colors come to mind, for example: Christmas: red and green; Fourth of July: red, white, and blue; Thanksgiving: brown and orange.

When you periodically visit your local quilt shop, the shelves will be filled with fabric for the upcoming holiday. Pick out one or two bolts and leave the collection. Pull the remaining fabric needed from the different color groups represented. Just like fashion, holiday fabric lines change from year to year, bringing a distinct look to each collection. If you work exclusively from one group, your quilt stands the chance of looking confusing.

Holiday. Can you find the corn in this Thanksgiving example?

Focus

Focus fabrics are large scale prints with many colors. Often you can find extremely unusual color combinations within one piece of fabric, or colors that have many different color variations; for example, a red/brown with a red/yellow. Once you have found your fabric, you must become a detective. Seek out different pieces of fabric which represent the colors in the focus fabric. Remember, this is the time to work with those unusual colors. One may end up being your next favorite color in the world! Wonderful focus fabrics are not always readily available, so keep a keen eye on the lookout for them.

Focus. Starting with unusual color combinations represented in your focus fabric will give you a more interesting quilt and teach you color confidence.

Le Moyne Star detail. Quilt shown on page 72.

Neutrals

We often think of neutrals as background fabric, but I have achieved stunning results working with white and off-white fabrics. Every time I visit my quilt shop I scan the neutral-colored fabrics. Since these fabrics are also vulnerable to current fabric trends, and often appear the same, you should look each season for new, interesting neutrals and invest in them. You can never have enough. It is an excellent way to learn the concept of light, medium, and dark.

Neutrals. Notice the range of values in this example: subtle but effective.

Friendship Star detail. Quilt shown on page 38.

Theme

Pictorial or theme fabrics are also called conversational or novelty prints. Season to season the subjects change. Flags might be big this year and birds the next. You might find stragglers from previous seasons to add to your collection. Novelty fabrics open the doors to creative storytelling through fabric. Two-and-one-half years ago, Lizzie came into our life. We are now dog lovers! I began to look for fabrics that related to dogs; one even included a dog-bone print. It was helpful that the fabrics had a common color that ran through all the different prints. This helped lend continuity to the collection. Novelties are a little tricky because they cannot be put into the category of light or dark. You need to include fabrics that are tone-on-tone, and not scattered with print. This gives the eye a resting place.

Theme. A tribute to Lizzie.

Tawanda detail. Quilt shown on page 32.

Historical

Quilts have been dated and documented throughout history by the fabrics used in them. If you are a history buff and find yourself drawn to a particular period of time, try duplicating the look with reproduction fabrics. For fun, sneak in some surprise fabrics to reward the viewer. This is a concentrated way to work and will require some study of old quilts. Check magazines and books for references.

Historical. These colors are indicative of the mid-1800s.

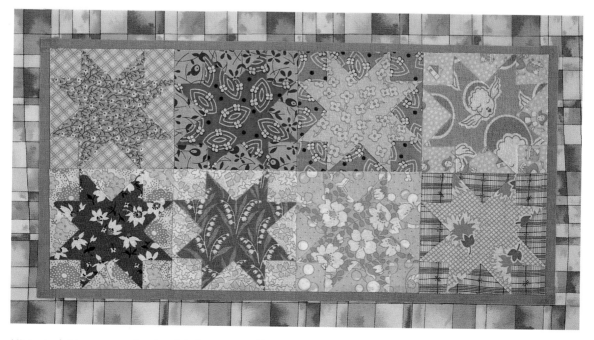

Historical. Many reproduction fabrics are readily available. These represent fabrics from the early to mid-1900s. The fabric in the upper-right star is from real feedsacks.

Monochromatic

Working in a monochromatic color scheme means working with just one color family. At first this might sound like the easiest way to work, but it can often be the most challenging. Fabrics in the medium color range are readily available, but finding fabrics in the light and dark ranges takes time and patience. I suggest you start collecting fabrics for this type of quilt well in advance. You need an equal amount of light, medium, and dark to make your stars "sing." And don't be afraid to use variations of the color.

Monochromatic. Variety and contrast are the keys to a successful monochromatic quilt.

Courage, brother! Do not stumble,
Though thy path be dark as night;
There's a star to guide the humble,
Trust in God and do the Right.

—Norman Macleod, 1872

Solids

Any quilt is stunning in solids. Unlike print fabrics, solids will test your piecing skills, since every mistake will show. Consider using a black background or possibly an all white background. The results will be crisp and clean.

Solids. The striped print inner border in this example is a welcomed surprise.

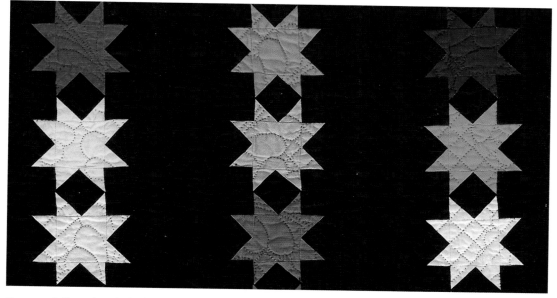

Sawtooth Star detail. Quilt shown on page 41.

Collections

Every season different fabric designers and manufacturers come out with new fabric collections. Each collection has a name and the prints are all made to complement each other, with guaranteed results. I am resistant to using them because they take the thinking and learning out of the process. However, I must admit there have been collections that have knocked my socks off, and in moments of weakness, I have purchased the entire set!

When working with a collection, start with the base fabrics and add fabrics that aren't in the set. This is how you get a unique look, something that has your name on it, not the designer's!

Collections. Vary the scale of print when working with a collection of fabrics.

Sun Ray detail. Quilt shown on page 58.

Scrap

Use it all! Approach each star in the quilt with a different set of fabric colors. Make every star look great on its own. Blocks should not be dependent on surrounding blocks. When ninety percent of the quilt is completed, look carefully for the color that seems to emerge the most. That color will most likely be your "comfort color." Repeat this color in the remaining stars for continuity. The greater the variety of color, diversity of print, and variation of light and dark, the more interesting the quilt will be. This is a very challenging and exciting way to work, and you will definitely be stretched as a quiltmaker when it comes time to put the blocks together.

Scrap. Make each block sparkle on its own and add your "comfort color" as I did with the blue fabric in this example.

Where shall we adventure, to-day that we're afloat,
Weary of the weather and steering by a star?
Shall it be to Africa, a-steering of the boat,
To Providence, or Babylon, or off to Malabar?

—Robert Louis Stevenson, 1894

Personal Challenge

While working on my first book, *Quilts for Fabric Lovers*, the foremost thought in my mind was that we should be able to work with any piece of fabric available to us. When my technical editor, Joyce Lytle, picked up on this, she presented me with a piece of fabric she had been blessed with. I really thought the only appropriate place for this fabric would be curtains for an RV. So I hung the fabric on my work wall and tried to ignore it.

Later, my challenge mini-group decided to put pieces of paper with colors written on them in a paper bag. We then had to pull out two colors and work with them in a quilt. Everyone thought it was quite humorous that I pulled purple and orange! Guess what? Joyce's fabric could save the day. I would use it as my focus fabric. What is so interesting is that when I share the story with a class of twenty people, at least two like the fabric. I have learned a valuable lesson in this experience: one person's horrible is another person's wonderful. Stretch yourself; walk through new color doors. You might be surprised by what you learn.

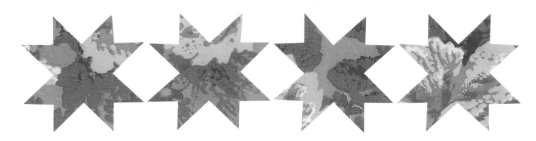

Challenge Fabric

Personal challenge met.

Working with Color

Once you have decided on the direction of your star quilt, there are a few rules to keep in mind when selecting fabric for your quilt. (I usually start with quarter-yard cuts of fifteen to twenty different fabrics, adding more from my existing collection as the quilt takes form.) The following guidelines will help you choose fabrics that work effectively in your quilts. Here are the basic rules I use in choosing fabrics. They have never failed me.

Value (Light to Dark)

Value is the lightness or darkness of a color. Most fabrics can be grouped into categories of light, medium, or dark. The exception to this generality are fabrics that have all three values in them such as novelty prints. It is important your quilt has a sufficient amount of each value to give the contrast needed to make your quilt sparkle.

To check this, when choosing fabrics line up the bolts or pieces of fabric and squint your eyes. You will be amazed how much of the fabric you have chosen will be in the medium range. Force yourself to put back some of the medium fabrics and add more light and dark. Light and dark fabrics are not usually the eye grabbers, and it requires discipline to add the not-so-exciting lights and darks. But your discipline will pay off when your stars shine bright!

Character of Print

Character of print refers to the size and scale or visual texture of a print. Every year fabric lines seem to have a new look and it often relates to the character of print. One year it might be floral and the next year geometric. For a truly exciting quilt it is important to mix and match several different looks. I love sneaking in fabrics not expected in the quilt. It gives a fresh and fun look.

Remember, a piece of fabric cuts up much differently than it looks on the bolt. To test this, squint your eyes again to see if the fabric character "reads" the same (biggest culprit: tone on tones). If two bolts do, eliminate one and add another with different character. Why purchase two pieces of fabric that are will look the same, when you can have two entirely different looking pieces?

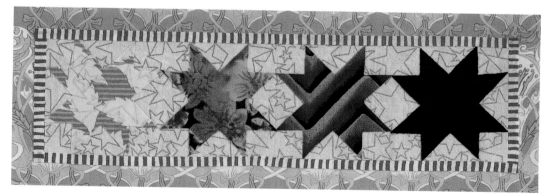

Light to dark values

Character of print

Color Families

Fabrics can be categorized into different color groups or families. Subdivisions occur depending on what colors are mixed in with the base color. Once you depart from the three primary colors, the world of color is unlimited.

Many people, like myself, have a hard time identifying subtle color variations. My mental picture of green might be entirely different from yours! When choosing fabrics and colors for my quilts, I have the personal motto, "Just use it all!" It is not vital to have each piece of fabric match perfectly. Incorporating fabrics with color variations works because we are making our star quilts of many fabrics. Transition fabrics act as a bridge between fabrics you would be reluctant to combine. Fabrics with many different colors represented in them work beautifully as transition fabrics.

When you visit your local quilt shop keep in mind that fabric, like fashion, has different looks and styles depending on the year and season! It's much like going to the clothing store and either being thrilled because you love it all, or frustrated because the look just isn't you! That is why I encourage quilters to visit their local quilt shop frequently, and seek out new stores when visiting other areas. This way you will develop and maintain an interesting stash of fabrics.

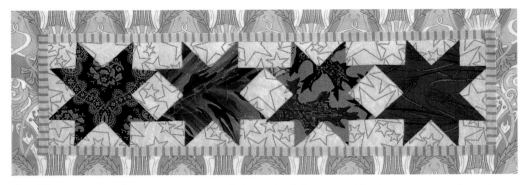

The fabrics used in the two center stars bridge the fabrics used in the stars on both ends.

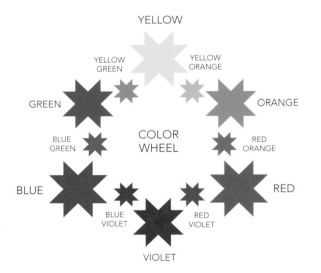

Primary Colors: red, yellow, and blue
These colors cannot be achieved by mixing other colors.
Secondary Colors: orange, green, and violet
These colors result when mixing two adjacent primary colors.
Tertiary Colors: yellow-orange, red-orange, red-violet, blue-violet, blue-green, yellow-green
These colors result when mixing two adjacent secondary colors.

Hue: another word for color
Tint: color + white
Tone: color + grey
Shade: color + black
Intensity or chroma: the brightness or dullness of a color
Value: the lightness or darkness of a color
Contrast: the difference in lightness and darkness between colors.

The Color Wheel

Using a color wheel can be an overwhelming experience for even the most seasoned quiltmaker. Words like hue, tint, value, and chroma can be confusing at best. It seems to me that either you are born with the ability to recognize subtle color distinctions or not. My daughter Adair has had the ability to arrange fabrics by intensity, value, tint, and shade, since she was very young. As for myself, it has taken many years of training. So why use a color wheel if it is only a source of frustration? Because there are many times when understanding color relationships can help you solve your design dilemmas.

If you are working in a monochromatic color scheme (working in just one color) and the quilt lacks sparkle, look to the opposite side of the color wheel and sprinkle in this color. This color combination is called *complementary*.

Another safe and pleasing way to work is with colors that appear next to each other on the wheel. This color combination is called *analogous*.

Last but not least, you can place an equilateral triangle on top of the color wheel and use the colors that meet the points. This color combination is called *triad*.

If you use the color wheel at its most basic and simple form, you might be surprised at how it will become your next best quilting tool.

A Sampling of Stars

By now I am certain you have a comfortable supply of fabric to start with. (Remember, you can keep adding new and unusual pieces until the last stitch is taken.) The star blocks used in each quilt project are listed in order of difficulty. Start at the beginning of the book and make a few 6" Friendship and 6" Sawtooth Stars. This is a good place to become familiar with both the principles of star making and your fabric stash (or fabric selection). Then proceed to the next star blocks, making them 12". Once you master the 12" star, try the 6" blocks, if the instructions are given (some of the blocks are too complicated for 6"). Feel free to add more fabric combinations than might be reflected in the directions. For example, if the diagram shows three different pieces of fabric, use five if possible. The stars can be as simple or as complicated as you want. Here are some tips to keep in mind as you create your own sampling of stars.

1. For a clean, crisp 12" star, choose the fabric for the star tip and the background first. They need to have the greatest contrast between light and dark. Then choose the remaining pieces of fabric for the star body. Each block needs to be regarded as a little masterpiece. Look at A and B at right.

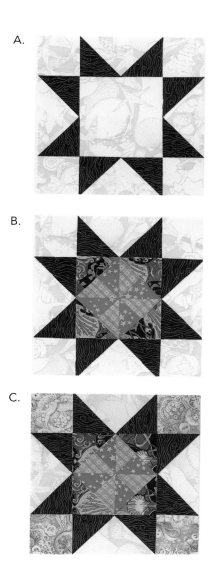

A.

B.

C.

2. When making a block, keep the background fabric the same. In an attempt to incorporate more fabric into the selected block, people sometimes use more than one for the background. In doing this you will lose the star tips. (Changing the background fabric is appropriate when repeating star blocks of the same size in a straight or diagonal set. Interesting secondary patterns will often occur.) Look at B and C above.

3. As you make the different star blocks, feel free to use many different background fabrics. Look at D and E.

Look at the difference between the stars with only one background fabric and those with many. (If you like the sample with only one background, it's OK; just stay open to new possibilities.) It's also fun to mix both light and dark background star blocks within the same quilt. This will keep your quilt from looking flat. Look at E and F.

D. Stars using one background fabric

E. Stars using different background fabrics

4. It is also OK to use both off-white and white in the same quilt. If you are uncomfortable doing this, look for neutral fabrics that have both white and off-white in them. They will act as a bridge, bringing both off-white and white together in the same quilt. Look at G.

5. Last, but not least...have fun! Stretch yourself. Use fabrics that make you uncomfortable. It's amazing how some of the ugliest stars still work in these quilts. If a star turns out just too ugly for words, we have quilt backs! Star quilts are an excellent way to expand and grow in your knowledge of fabric and design.

F. Reversing lights and darks in stars and background fabrics

G. White and off-white in the same fabric

STAR GALLERY

The moving moon went up the sky,
And nowhere did abide;
Softly she was going up,
A star or two beside.

—Samuel Taylor Coleridge

Welcome to the Star Gallery. The following quilts are combinations of many of the different stars presented in this book. The quilts are made up of either six-inch or twelve-inch blocks, just perfect for a sampler. This is a fun way to experience and learn the piecing challenges of the stars in this book without committing to an entire quilt of just one star. I have taught a class based on this idea for several years and the quilts in this section are the results of this workshop. Quilters come wanting to learn the technical aspects of piecing stars and are pleasantly surprised when they realize the fabric knowledge they acquire. Keep in mind you must have an adventurous spirit. This quilt will take you in directions uncharted! I am always amazed at the interpretation of the stars.

Santa Maria Stars, 52" x 52"; pieced and hand quilted by Linda J. Estrada

Mind Blowing Stars, 73" x 91"; pieced and machine quilted by Nancy Elliott MacDonald

It's a Blast!
73" x 58";
pieced and
machine quilted
by Cynthia K. Slyker

Star Quilt, 64" x 64";
pieced by Maureen Weber-Atteberry
and machine quilted by Sandy Klop

The Dead Fish Quilt,
64" x 54"; pieced by
Leslie J. Skibo and
machine quilted by
Rhondi Hindman

Are the Stars Out Tonite?,
78" x 80"; pieced and machine
quilted by Gloria Lynne Smith.
Photography by Mellisa Karlin
Mahoney, courtesy of Quilter's®
Newsletter Magazine.

A Quilt for Christmas, 52½" x 57";
pieced by Emma Allebes and
machine quilted by Barbara Wilson

North Star, 54" x 54";
pieced by Patti Scott-Baier
and hand quilted by
Mary Bertken

Summer Sky, 52" x 66";
pieced and hand quilted
by Linda K. Cover

Christmas Time, 44" x 44";
pieced and hand quilted
by Alex Anderson

Stars, 54" x 70";
pieced and machine quilted
by Melanie Bobbitt

Tawanda, 48" x 48";
pieced and hand quilted
by Alex Anderson

Star Studded, 52" x 64";
pieced by Lyn Oser Mann
and machine quilted by
Teri Dowdee

Jordan's Star, 54" x 54";
pieced and hand quilted
by Leslie Ison

Prairie Stars, 48" x 60"; pieced and hand quilted by Sally Barlow

Chine Du, 60" x 74"; pieced and machine quilted by Blanche Young

Pat and Alex and Me, 66" x 72"; pieced and hand quilted by Rosemary Houser

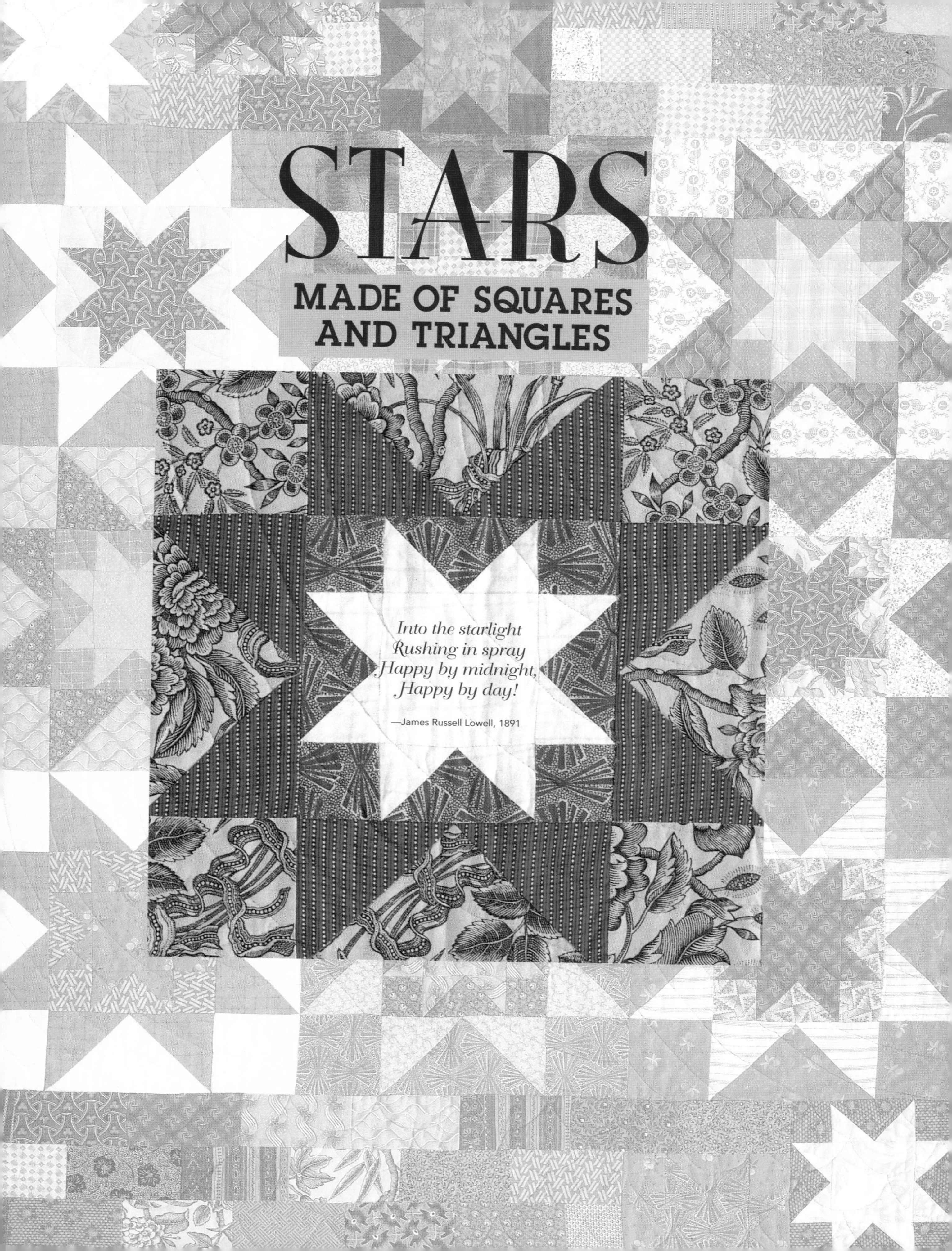

STARS

MADE OF SQUARES AND TRIANGLES

Into the starlight
Rushing in spray
Happy by midnight,
Happy by day!

—James Russell Lowell, 1891

Friendship Star

Alex Anderson; machine quilted by Susanne M. Rasmussen
This quilt is 56" x 64" and contains forty 6" Friendship Stars and seventy-six 4" Pinwheels.

Fabric Tips

Neutrals are often used as background fabrics. Season to season the fabrics change and I can't bear leaving the quilt store without just a bit of this and that! Needless to say, my collection of neutrals is not for the light-hearted. I have found making a quilt using whites and off-whites can produce stunning results. The key to this quilt is making sure white is included; otherwise, your quilt will lack sparkle. Notice that a few very light pastels are included; this helps tie in the unusual inner border. The range of values between the white and medium can be as narrow or as broad as you want. The greater the variety of fabrics used, the more successful your quilt will be.

Fabric Requirements

The following instructions give the total yardage needed to complete your quilt. (See General Instructions: Yardage, page 8.)

   White: ½ yard
   Off-White: 2 yards
   Medium: 1¼ yards
   Inner Border: 2 yards
   Backing: 4 yards

6" Friendship Star

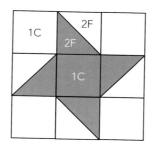

CUTTING

Traditional: use template patterns 1C, 2F.

The following numbers are for one Friendship Star. You will need forty in all. (See General Instructions: Cutting, page 8.)

Star Body
◆ Cut one 2½" square (1C).
◆ Cut two 2⅞" squares, then cut ◱ (2F).

Star Background
◆ Cut two 2⅞" squares, then cut ◱ (2F).
◆ Cut four 2½" squares (1C).

PIECING AND PRESSING

Follow the diagram below for piecing sequence. The arrows indicate which way to press. (See Pressing, page 10.)

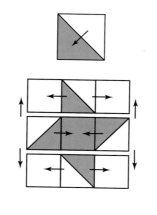

4" Pinwheels and 2" Half-Square Triangles

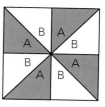

CUTTING

Traditional: use template pattern 2F.

The following numbers are for one Pinwheel. You will need seventy-six in all. (See General Instructions: Cutting, page 8.)

Triangle A
◆ Cut two 2⅞" squares, then cut ◱ (2F).

Triangle B
◆ Cut two 2⅞" squares, then cut ◱ (2F).

PIECING AND PRESSING

Follow the diagram below for piecing sequence. Use the same cutting numbers for half-square triangles as for the Pinwheels. Press to the darker fabric.

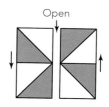

Setting

Arrange the blocks as shown in diagram. This quilt is constructed of blocks that are multiples of 2". You must approach this like a jig-saw puzzle. (Some people are more comfortable cutting pieces of graph paper to scale and laying them out on paper first.) When you have different block sizes in a quilt, don't be afraid to use the Y seam (shown on page 73) to complete the construction. Piece the quilt body.

Inner Border

◆ Cut two strips of fabric 4½" wide by at least 56".
◆ Cut two strips of fabric 4½" wide by at least 64".

1. Sew on the inner border. The inner border has mitered corners. This technique was used to enhance the look of the border fabric. See your basic quiltmaking book for instructions on this technique.

2. Sew on the 4" Pinwheels as your last border. Congratulations, your Friendship Star quilt is ready to layer, baste, quilt, and possibly pick up a few autographs from your favorite quilters!

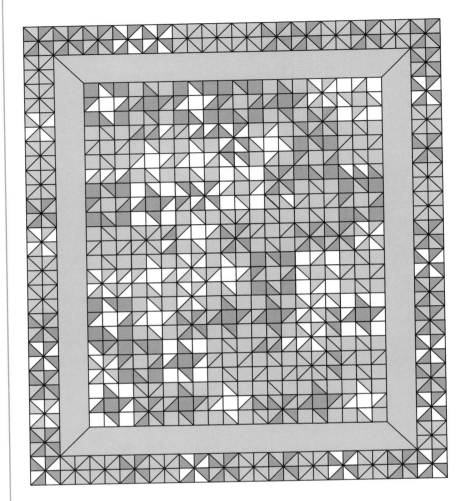

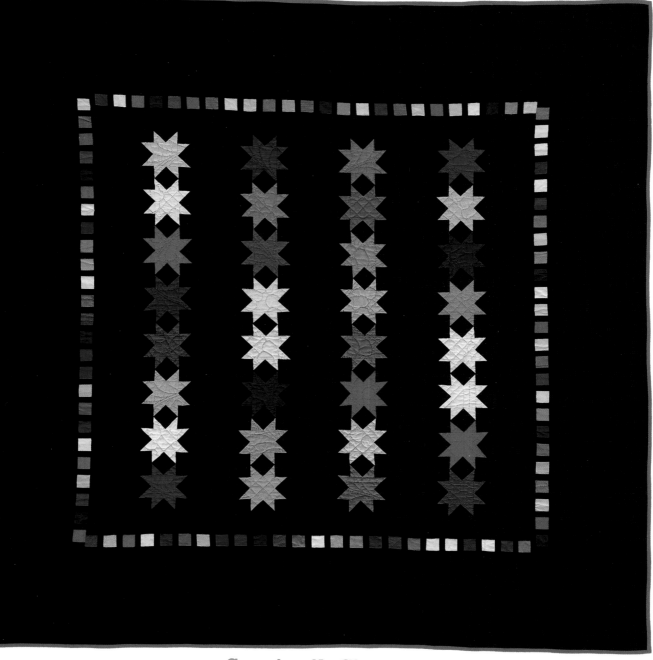

Sawtooth Star

Pieced and hand quilted by Alex Anderson
This quilt is 75" x 75" and contains thirty-two 6" Sawtooth Stars.

Fabric Tips

When working with solid colored fabrics, remember to include some very light pastels and yellow for sparkle. The greater the variety of colors and values you use, the more interesting your quilt will be.

Fabric Requirements

The following instructions give the total yardage needed to complete your quilt. (See General Instructions: Yardage, page 8.)

Stars: 1¾ yards (includes yardage for inner border)

Background: 5½ yards (includes yardage for borders)

Backing: 4¼ yards

6" Sawtooth Star

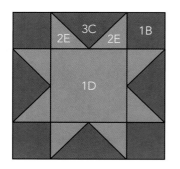

CUTTING

Traditional: use template patterns 1D, 2E, 3C, 1B.

The following numbers are for one Sawtooth Star. You will need thirty-two in all. (See General Instructions: Cutting, page 8.)

Star Body

◆ Cut one 3½" square (1D).
◆ Cut four 2⅜" squares, then cut ◻ (2E).

Background

Important: Cut the star body background and inner border strips first. From the remaining fabric, cut the outer border and sashing from the length of the fabric so you won't have to piece them. You will have fabric left over.

◆ Cut one 4¼" square, then cut ⊠ (3C).
◆ Cut four 2" squares (1B).

PIECING AND PRESSING

Follow the diagram below for piecing sequence. The ^ indicates which edge or point to line up (see All-Star Lineup, pages 8-9). The arrows indicate which way to press (see Pressing, page 10).

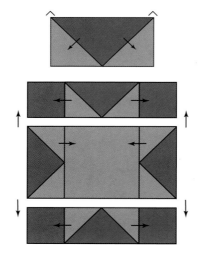

Sashing

◆ Cut five strips of background fabric 6½" x 48½" for vertical sashing between the stars.
◆ Cut two strips of background fabric 3½" x 54½" for horizontal sashing.

Inner Border

◆ Cut six strips of background fabric 1½" wide. Cut the strips four times so they measure about 15" long.
◆ Cut several strips of star body fabrics 2" x 15".

Outer Border

◆ Cut two strips of background fabric 9½" x 57½" for outside vertical border.
◆ Cut two strips of background fabric 9½" x 75½" for outside horizontal border.

Setting

1. Arrange four rows of eight stars. Make sure the light stars are sprinkled across the entire quilt. Sew the rows together.
2. Alternate and sew the five '6½" x 48½' sashing strips with the four rows of stars.
3. Sew the two 3½" x 54½" sashing strips on the top and bottom.
4. Alternate and strip sew the 1½" x 15" inner border strips and 2" x 15" star body fabrics together and press. Mix and match the colored strips into several groups.

Cut into 2" wide strips.

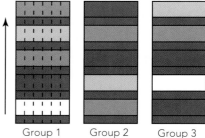

Group 1   Group 2   Group 3

5. Cut these pieced units into 2" strips.

6. Connect the strips into two rows of 54½". Sew to the top and bottom of the quilt top.

7. Connect the remaining strips into two rows of 57½". Sew to the two sides of the quilt.

8. Sew on the outer border. Your Sawtooth Star quilt is ready to quilt. If you have used solid fabrics, consider using a traditional quilting design. This quilt lends itself beautifully to intricate quilting. Have fun. I did!

Connect   Connect

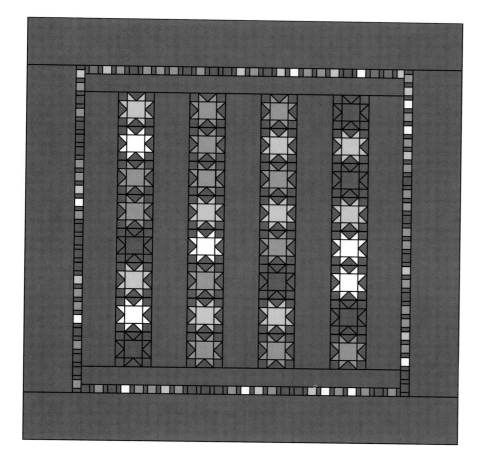

Double Sawtooth Star

Alex Anderson; machine quilted by Susanne M. Rasmussen
This quilt is 52" x 52" and contains nine 12" Double Sawtooth Stars and eleven 6" Sawtooth Stars.

Fabric Tips

The selection of fabric for this quilt was inspired by the Smithsonian fabric collection. When starting with a specific collection, feel free to include other fabrics that are not in the collection you are working with. This gives the quilt unique character. Keep in mind this is a scrap quilt, without specific light or dark color placement of the star body and background. "Mix and match" is the name of the game. Have fun!

Fabric Requirements

The following instructions give the total yardage needed to complete your quilt. (See General Instructions: Yardage, page 8.)

Stars: 1½ yards
Background: 2 yards
Border: 1½ yards
Backing: 3¼ yards

6" Sawtooth Star

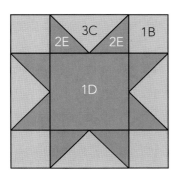

CUTTING

Traditional: use template patterns 1D, 2E, 3C, 1B.

The following numbers are for one 6" Sawtooth Star. You will need eleven in all. (See General Instructions: Cutting, page 8.)

Star Body
- ◆ Cut one 3½" square (1D).
- ◆ Cut four 2⅜" squares, then cut ◩ (2E).

Background
- ◆ Cut one 4¼" square, then cut ⊠ (3C).
- ◆ Cut four 2" squares (1B).

PIECING AND PRESSING

Follow the diagram below for piecing sequence. The ^ indicates which edge or point to line up (see All-Star Lineup, pages 8-9). The arrows indicate which way to press (see Pressing, page 10).

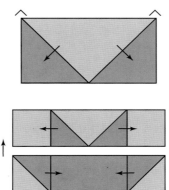

12" Double Sawtooth Star

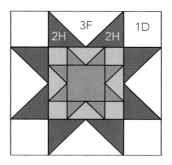

CUTTING

Traditional: use template patterns 2H, 3F, 1D.

The cutting numbers are for one 12" Double Sawtooth Star. You will need nine in all. Cut and piece the 6" inner star as before.

Star Body
- ◆ Cut four 3⅞" squares, then cut ◩ (2H).

Background
- ◆ Cut one 7¼" square, then cut ⊠ (3F).
- ◆ Cut four 3½" squares (1D).

PIECING AND PRESSING

Follow the diagram below for piecing sequence. The arrows indicate which way to press (see Pressing, page 10).

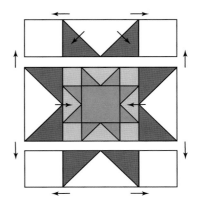

Border

The border is made up of the eleven previously pieced 6" stars and one hundred thirty-seven 2" x 4" rectangles. Feel free to add more fabrics from the same color families you have already used to make the stars. This is how you get the scrap look. Notice how the rectangles are primarily the darker pieces of fabric, with just a few light rectangles placed randomly throughout the entire border.

Rectangles

Traditional: use template pattern 2A.

◆ Cut one hundred thirty-seven 2½" x 4½" rectangles (2A). It is important to use this exact size so the quilt will fit together mathematically when you incorporate the 6" stars.

Setting

1. Arrange your blocks as shown in diagram.
2. Join your blocks in a straight set.
3. Place the rectangles around the 36" center along with the eleven 6" stars previously made. Notice the rectangles are staggered exactly in half.
4. Sew on the border.
Congratulations! Your Double Sawtooth Star wall hanging is ready to layer, baste, and quilt. I hope your star quilt looks as wonderful in your home as this quilt does in mine!

Variable Star

Alex Anderson; hand quilted by Mary Hershberger
This quilt is 59¼" x 59¼" and contains thirty-six 6" Variable Stars.

Fabric Tips

The background alternate-block fabric is made up of an identical print in two colorways. This unusual set gave this quilt an old look. Always consider introducing white into a quilt. It's OK to mix beige and white together; it keeps the quilt from looking muddy. Use as many different blues and reds as you can; don't worry if there are variations within each color family. This adds interest.

Fabric Requirements

The following instructions give the total yardage needed to complete your quilt. (See General Instructions: Yardage, page 8.)

Star and Sawtooth Border: 2 yards

Star Background: 1¼ yards

Alternate Block Background: 2¼ yards

Inner Border: ¼ yard

Backing: 3¾ yards

6" Variable Star

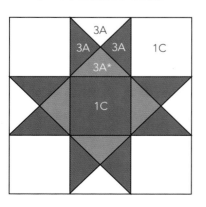

CUTTING

Traditional: use template patterns 1C, 3A.

The following numbers are for one Variable Star. You will need thirty-six in all. (See General Instructions: Cutting, page 8.)

Star Body
- Cut one 2½" square (1C).
- Cut two 3¼" squares, then cut ⊠ (3A).
- Cut one 3¼" square of a different fabric, then cut ⊠ (3A*).

Background
- Cut one 3¼" square, then cut ⊠ (3A).
- Cut four 2½" squares (1C).

PIECING AND PRESSING

Follow the diagram below for piecing sequence. The ^ indicates which edge or point to line up (see All-Star Lineup, pages 8-9). The arrows indicate which way to press (see Pressing, page 10).

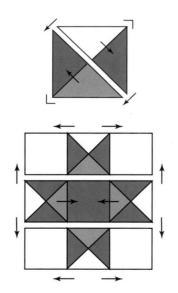

Inner Border

Several fabrics have been used. Notice the color change in relationship to the pieced border. The two primary colors used are set opposite from each other.
- Cut two strips 1½" x 51½".
- Cut two strips 1½" x 53½".

Outer Border

Traditional: use template pattern 2D, 1M.
- Cut thirty-five 4" squares of star fabric, then cut ◩ (2D).
- Cut thirty-five 4" squares of alternate block fabrics, then cut ◩ (2D).

Make seventy half-square triangle units.

- Cut two 3⅝" alternate block fabric squares (1M).

Alternate Blocks

Traditional: use template pattern 1G.

Cut twenty-five 6½" squares of alternate block fabric (1G).

Notice the arrangement of the two background colorways.

Side Quarter Triangles

- Cut five 9¾" squares from the two alternate block fabrics (4 of one color and 1 of the other color), then cut ⊠. (No template pattern given.)

Corner Triangles

◆ Cut two $5\frac{1}{8}$" squares of the alternate block fabric, then cut ◻. (No template pattern given.)

Setting

1. Arrange your stars and alternate blocks in a pleasing layout. Remember they are set on point.

2. Join the blocks and the side and corner triangles in a diagonal set.

3. Sew on the inner border.

4. Sew together seventeen half-square triangles for side border. Repeat. Sew together eighteen half-square triangles for top border and add the $3\frac{5}{8}$" alternate block fabric square to one end. Repeat for bottom border. Sew on the outer border.

Celebrate! Your quilt is ready to layer, baste, and quilt...just in time for the Fourth of July.

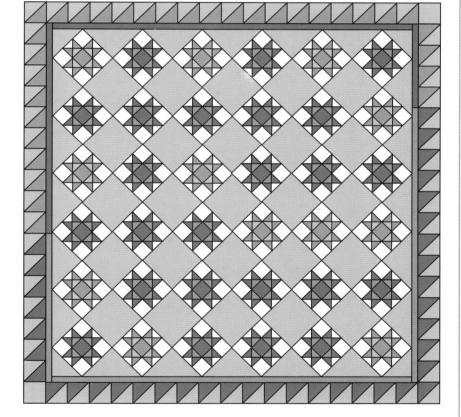

12" Variable Star Variation

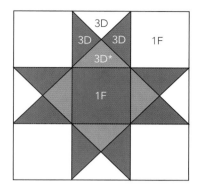

Traditional: use template patterns 1F, 3D.

Star Body

◆ Cut one $4\frac{1}{2}$" square (1F).
◆ Cut two $5\frac{1}{4}$" squares, then cut ⊠ (3D).
◆ Cut one $5\frac{1}{4}$" square of a different fabric, then cut ⊠ (3D*).

Background

◆ Cut one $5\frac{1}{4}$" square, then cut ⊠ (3D).
◆ Cut four $4\frac{1}{2}$" squares (1F).

Swamp Angel

Alex Anderson; machine quilted by Susanne M. Rasmussen
This quilt is 60" x 66" and contains seventy-six 6" Swamp Angel stars.

Fabric Tips

The fabrics for this quilt came from a great piece of focus fabric. I chose it because my fabric collection lacked purple and teal. What is more interesting is that this particular piece of fabric was never actually used in the pieced top. It was merely employed as a color reference. When you find a great piece of focus fabric, you should purchase at least a few yards, since it could become the border, or as in this case, the perfect piece for the back!

Fabric Requirements

The following instructions give the total yardage needed to complete your quilt. (See General Instructions: Yardage, page 8.)

Stars: 4¼ yards

Background: 2½ yards

Backing: 4 yards

6" Swamp Angel

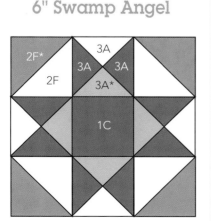

CUTTING

Traditional: use template patterns 1C, 3A, 2F.

The following numbers are for one Swamp Angel. You will need seventy-six in all. (See General Instructions: Cutting, page 8.)

Star Body

- Cut one 2½" square (1C).
- Cut two 3¼" squares, then cut ⊠ (3A).
- Cut one 3¼" square of a different fabric, then cut ⊠ (3A*).

Background

- Cut one 3¼" square, then cut ⊠ (3A).
- Cut two 2⅞" squares, then cut ◺ (2F).
- Cut two 2⅞" squares from star fabric, then cut ◺ (2F*).

PIECING AND PRESSING

Follow the diagram below for piecing sequence. The arrows indicate which way to press (see Pressing, page 10).

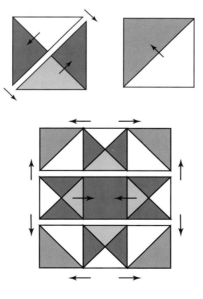

Inner and Outer Border

You will need one hundred thirty-six 3" squares-on-point blocks.

Traditional: use template patterns 1J, 2E.

- Cut one hundred thirty-six 2⅝" squares (1J).
- Cut two hundred seventy-two 2⅜" squares, then cut ◺ (2E).

PIECING AND PRESSING

Follow the diagram below for piecing sequence. The arrows indicate which way to press (see Pressing, page 10).

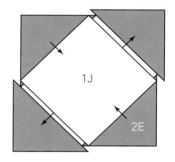

Setting

1. Arrange your blocks as shown.
2. Join the blocks in a straight set.
3. Sew on the inner-square-on-point border.
4. Sew on the star border.
5. Sew on the outer square on point border.

Congratulations! Your efforts have paid off; this simple block produced stunning results. Your quilt is ready to layer, baste, and quilt.

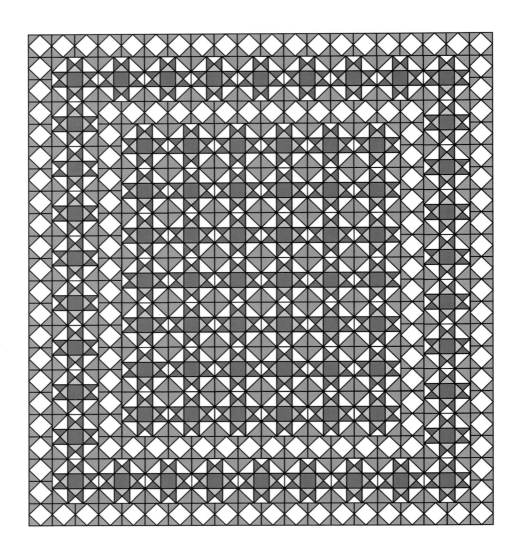

12" Swamp Angel Variation

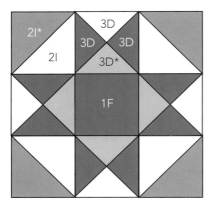

Traditional: use template patterns 1F, 3D, 2I.

Star Body
◆ Cut one 4½" square (1F).
◆ Cut two 5¼" squares, then cut ⊠ (3D).
◆ Cut one 5¼" square of a different fabric, then cut ⊠ (3D*).

Background
◆ Cut one 5¼" square, then cut ⊠ (3D).
◆ Cut two 4⅞" squares, then cut ◿ (2I).
◆ Cut two 4⅞" squares from star fabric, then cut ◿ (2I*)

Martha Washington Star

Alex Anderson; machine quilted by Susanne M. Rasmussen
This quilt is 76" x 82" and contains twenty-five 12" Martha Washington Stars and ten 6" Sawtooth Stars.

Fabric Tips

You never know where you will find color or design inspiration for your next quilt. Last year, while attending a quilt jamboree in Sacramento, California, a vision of color crossed the lawn. I had never seen this color represented so vibrantly in fiber before. It was knit into the most delightful sweater a person could possibly own. And who was the owner? Doreen Speckmann! I asked her where she had acquired this sweater and, of course, she had hand knit it. Well, that left me in a pinch.

Imagine how amazed and excited I was when I found, visiting my local quilt shop, a bolt of fabric that represented this same color of peach. I needed this fabric! Although I did not know how I would use it, I pulled out my color wheel and looked directly across to find its complementary color—green. Complementary combinations always work. If your quilt is looking a little monotonous, remember this trick; it works every time. Also notice the background fabrics are not all light. If your quilt is looking a little flat, consider reversing the background to dark and the star to light.

Fabric Requirements

The following instructions give the total yardage needed to complete your quilt. (See General Instructions: Yardage, page 8)

Stars: 3 yards
Background: 2¾ yards

Inner Border: ⅜ yard
Outer Border: 2¼ yards
Backing: 4¾ yards

12" Martha Washington Star

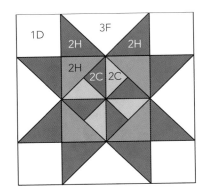

CUTTING

Traditional: use template patterns 2H, 2C, 3F, 1D.

The following numbers are for one 12" Martha Washington Star. You will need twenty-five in all. (See General Instructions: Cutting, page 8.)

Star Body
- Cut four 3⅞" squares, then cut ◨ (2H).
- Cut two 3" squares, then cut ◨ (2C). Repeat with another fabric.
- Cut two 3⅞" squares, then cut ◨ (2H).

Background
- Cut one 7¼" square, then cut ⊠ (3F).
- Cut four 3½" squares (1D).

PIECING AND PRESSING

Follow the diagram at right for piecing sequence. The arrows indicate which way to press (see Pressing, page 10).

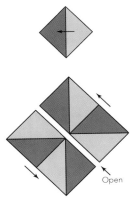

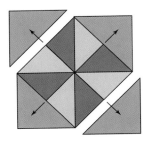

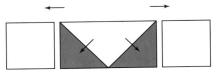

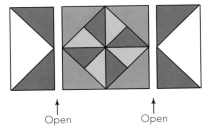

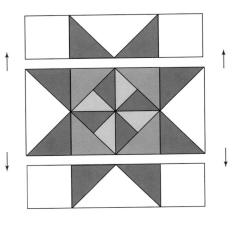

6" Sawtooth Star

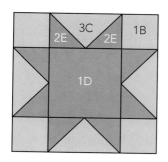

CUTTING

Traditional: use template patterns 1D, 2E, 3C, 1B.

The following numbers are for one Sawtooth Star. You will need ten in all. (See General Instructions: Cutting, page 8.)

Star Body
◆ Cut one 3½" square (1D).
◆ Cut four 2⅜" squares, then cut ◪ (2E).

Background
◆ Cut one 4¼" square, then cut ⊠ (3C).
◆ Cut four 2" squares (1B).

PIECING AND PRESSING

Follow the diagram below for piecing sequence. The ^ indicates which edge or point to line up (see All-Star Lineup, pages 8-9). The arrows indicate which way to press (see Pressing, page 10).

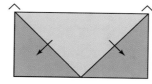

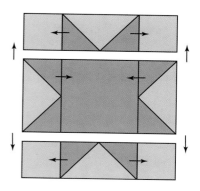

Inner Border

◆ Cut two strips 1½" x 66½".
◆ Cut two strips 1½" x 62½".

Outer Border

◆ Cut two strips 7½" x 68½".
◆ Cut two strips 7½" x 76½".

Setting

1. Arrange your blocks as shown in diagram.

2. Join your blocks in a straight set.

3. Sew on the inner border. Add sides first, then top and bottom.

4. Sew on the outer border. Add sides first, then top and bottom.

You did it! Your quilt is now ready to layer, baste, and quilt.

Pieced and machine quilted by Alex Anderson

12" Best of All

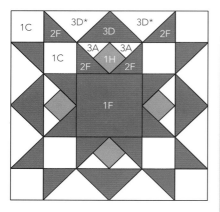

CUTTING

Traditional: use template patterns 1F, 1H, 3D, 2F, 1C, 3A.

Star Body

◆ Cut one $4\frac{1}{2}$" square (1F).
◆ Cut four $1\frac{7}{8}$" squares (1H).
◆ Cut one $5\frac{1}{4}$" square, then cut ⊠ (3D).
◆ Cut eight $2\frac{7}{8}$" squares, then cut ◻ (2F).

Background

◆ Cut eight $2\frac{1}{2}$" squares (1C).
◆ Cut two $3\frac{1}{4}$" squares, then cut ⊠ (3A).
◆ Cut two $5\frac{1}{4}$" squares of a different fabric, then cut ⊠ (3D*).

PIECING AND PRESSING

Follow the diagram below for piecing sequence. The ^ indicates which edge or point to line up (see All-Star Lineup, pages 8-9). The arrows indicate which way to press (see Pressing, page 10).

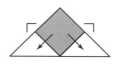

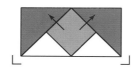

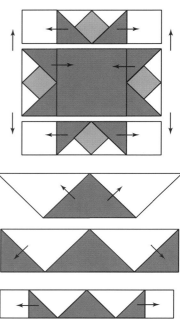

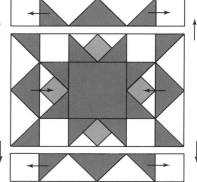

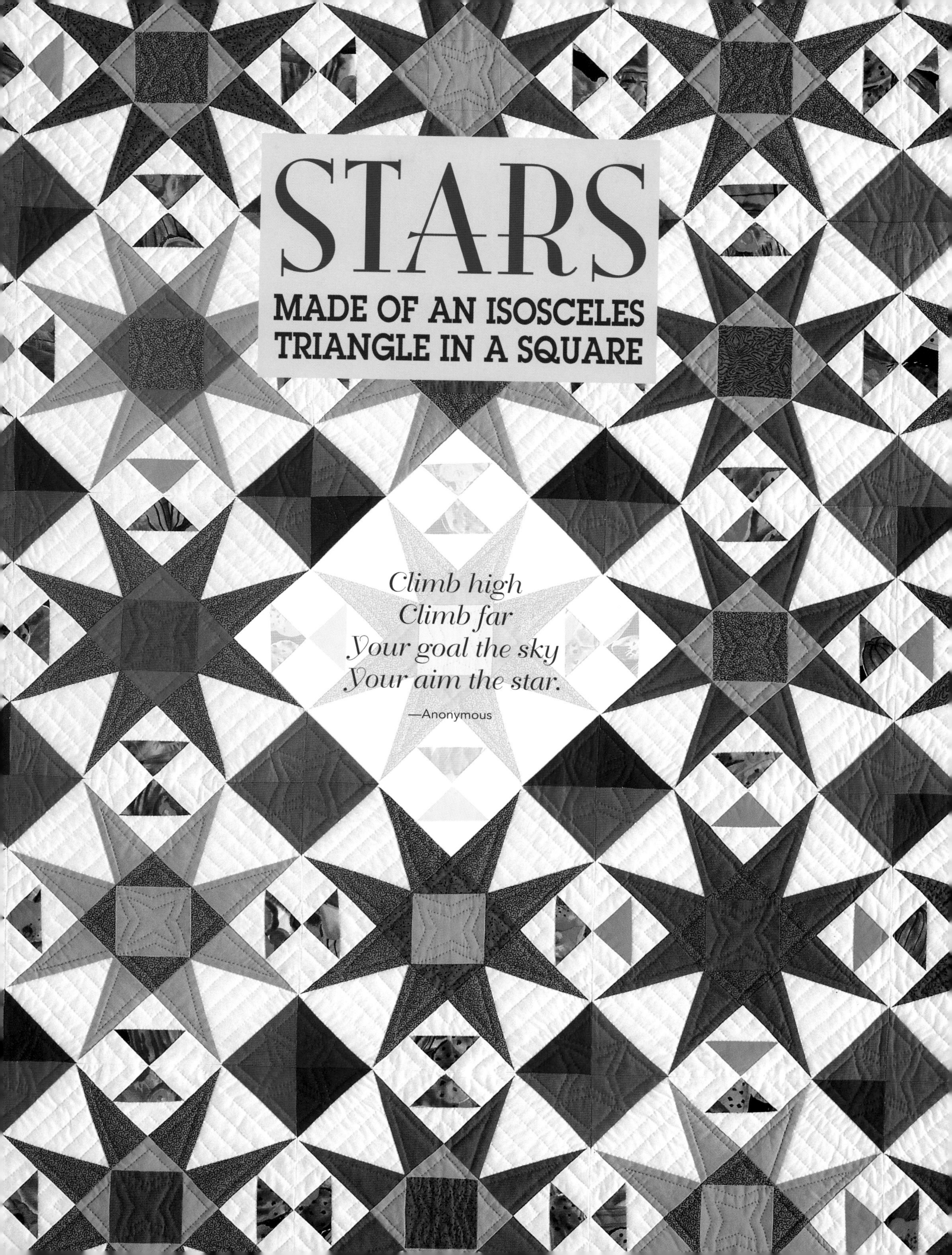

STARS

MADE OF AN ISOSCELES TRIANGLE IN A SQUARE

Climb high
Climb far
Your goal the sky
Your aim the star.
—Anonymous

Sun Ray

Alex Anderson; machine quilted by Susanne M. Rasmussen
This quilt is 58" x 62" and contains fifty-six 6" and sixteen 3" Sun Ray stars.

Fabric Tips

Stripes and polka dots are the best! I love putting them into my quilts. When I saw this group of fabrics I knew it had my name written all over it. I usually shy away from working with an entire collection because the quilts made entirely from these fabrics can end up looking prepackaged. However, you can solve this dilemma by introducing other fabrics into the set. In this case, I chose to add solids and a few pieces of black and white fabric. Even on the gloomiest day this quilt puts a smile on my face!

Fabric Requirements

The following instructions give the total yardage needed to complete your quilt. (See General Instructions: Yardage, page 8.)

Stars: 2 yards
Background: 2¾ yards
Inner Border: ¼ yard
Outer Border: 1½ yards
Backing: 4 yards

6" Sun Ray

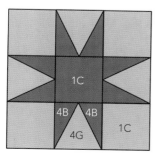

CUTTING

Traditional: use template patterns 1C, 4B, 4G.

The following numbers are for one 6" Sun Ray star. You will need fifty-six in all. (See General Instructions: Cutting, page 8.)

Star Body

◆ Cut one 2½" square (1C).
◆ Cut a strip 1¾" by at least 13¼". Fold and press end to end, like sides together. Cut two rectangles 1¾" x 3¼". Then cut on the diagonal as shown (4B).

Background

◆ Cut four 2⅞" squares, then cut as shown. (This cut produces a lot of waste. If fabric conservation is important, please use template pattern 4G.)

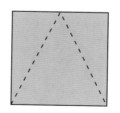

◆ Cut four 2½" squares (1C).

PIECING AND PRESSING

Follow the diagram below for piecing sequence. The ^ indicates which edge or point to line up (see All-Star Lineup, pages 8-9). The arrows indicate which way to press (see Pressing, page 10).

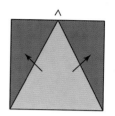

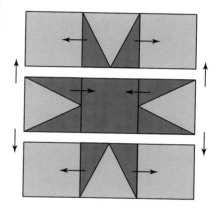

3" Sun Ray

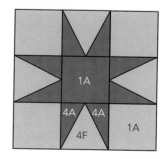

CUTTING

Traditional: use template patterns 1A, 4A, 4F.

The following numbers are for one 3" Sun Ray star. You will need sixteen in all. (see General Instructions: Cutting, page 8.)

Star Body

◆ Cut one 1½" square (1A).
◆ Cut a strip 1¼" by at least 9½". Fold and press end to end, like sides together. Cut two rectangles 1¼" x 2¼". Then cut on the diagonal as shown (4A).

Background

◆ Cut four 1⅞" squares, then cut as shown. (This cut produces a lot of waste. If fabric conservation is important please use template pattern 4F.)

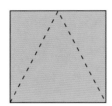

◆ Cut four 1½" squares (1A).

PIECING AND PRESSING

Follow the diagram below for piecing sequence. The ^ indicates which edge or point to line up (see All-Star Lineup, pages 8-9). The arrows indicate which way to press (see Pressing page 10).

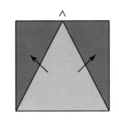

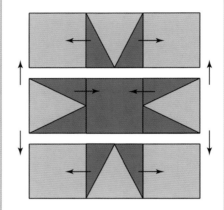

Inner Border

The inner border is two different widths in order to accommodate the outer border which is made up of 2" blocks.

◆ Cut two strips 1" x 48½".
◆ Cut two strips 1½" x 46½".

Outer Border

Traditional: use template pattern 1C.

◆ Cut three hundred twenty-four 2½" squares (1C).

Setting

1. Arrange your blocks as shown.
2. Join your blocks in a straight set, row by row.
3. Sew on the inner borders, making sure the narrow strips are on the side and the wide strips are on the top and bottom.
4. Sew on the outer checked border.

This quilt was a lot of fun to make. I hope it puts a smile on your face, the way this quilt does on mine!

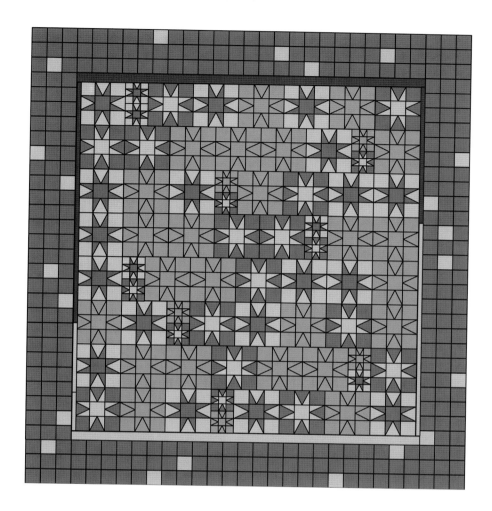

54-40 or Fight

Alex Anderson; machine quilted by Susanne M. Rasmussen
This quilt is 51" x 51" and contains forty-one 6" 54-40 or Fight stars and twenty 6" Double Nine Patch blocks.

Fabric Tips

Plaids never had a strong position in my fabric collection. So I was amazed one day when I left the quilt store with fifty dollars worth of plaid fat quarters in my pocket and no real plan in mind. Over time the fabric began to grow on me, and it was time to cut. As the quilt progressed, my fingers itched to add non-plaid fabrics. Letting intuition take over, I sneaked in several prints. I love this quilt.

Through the process of working with these fabrics, I have grown extremely fond of plaids and now seek them out on a regular basis. Always feel free to work with fabrics that take you out of your comfort zone; this is how you will grow as a quiltmaker.

Fabric Requirements

The following instructions give the total yardage needed to complete your quilt. (See General Instructions: Yardage, page 8.)

Red: 2 yards

Blue: 2 yards

Background: 2 ¾ yards

Backing: 3 yards

6" 54-40 or Fight

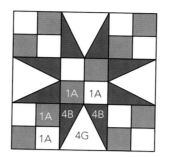

CUTTING

Traditional: use template patterns 4B, 4G, 1A.

The following numbers are for one 6" 54-40 or Fight star. You will need forty-one in all. (See General Instructions: Cutting, page 8.)

Star Body

◆ Cut a strip 1¾" by at least 13¼". Fold and press end to end, like sides together. Cut two rectangles 1¾" x 3¼". Then cut on the diagonal as shown (4B).

Background

◆ Cut four 2⅞" squares, then cut as shown. (This cut produces a lot of waste. If fabric conservation is important, please use template pattern 4G.)

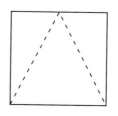

Four Patch

◆ Cut a strip of red 1½" by at least 15½".
◆ Cut a strip of background 1½" by at least 15½".

Sew the two strips together. Press to red. Cut off 1½" units (1A). Arrange and sew to create a Four Patch.

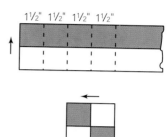

PIECING AND PRESSING

Follow the diagram below for piecing sequence. The ^ indicates which edge or point to line up (see All-Star Lineup, pages 8-9). The arrows indicate which way to press (see Pressing, page 10).

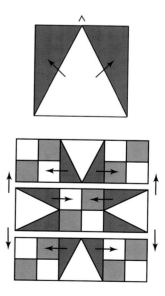

6" Double Nine Patch

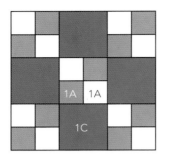

CUTTING

Traditional: use template patterns 1C, 1A.

The following numbers are for one 6" Double Nine Patch. You will need twenty in all. (See General Instructions: Cutting, page 8.)

- ◆ Cut four 2½" squares (1C).
- ◆ Cut a strip of red 1½" by at least 15½".
- ◆ Cut a strip of background 1½" by at least 15½".

Sew the two strips together. Press toward red. Cut off 1½" units (1A). Arrange and sew to create a Four Patch.

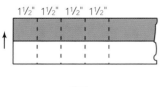

PIECING AND PRESSING

Follow the diagram below for piecing sequence. The arrows indicate which way to press (see Pressing, page 10). Note how the rotation of the Four Patch is changed in each of the four corners.

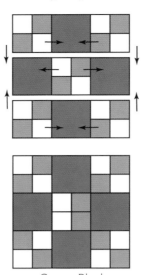

Corner Block

Side Quarter Triangles

Cut five 9¾" squares, then cut ⊠. (No template pattern given.)

Corner Triangles

Cut two 5⅛" squares, then cut ◩. (No template pattern given.)

Setting

1. Arrange your blocks as shown. Note the star blocks are set on point and each row is rotated to create the chain effect.

2. Join the pieced blocks and the side and corner triangles in a diagonal set.

Your star quilt is now ready to layer, baste, and quilt. I hope you have grown to love plaids as I do!

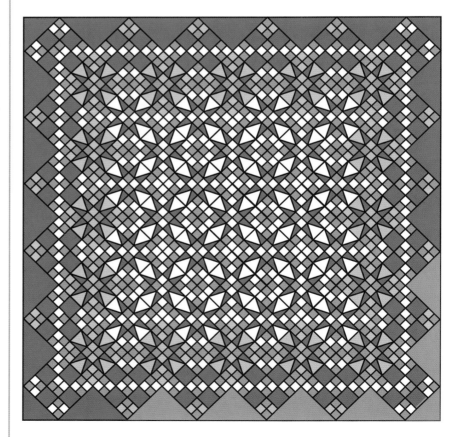

12" 54-40 or Fight Variation

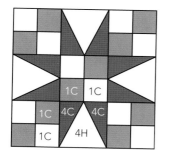

Traditional: use template patterns 4C, 4H, 1C.

Star Body

◆ Cut a strip 2¾" by at least 22". Fold and press end to end, like sides together. Cut two rectangles 2¾" x 5¼". Then cut on the diagonal as shown (4C).

Background

◆ Cut four 4⅞" squares, then cut as shown. (This cut produces a lot of waste. If fabric conservation is important, use template pattern 4H.)

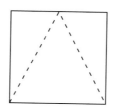

Four Patch

◆ Cut a strip of red 2½" by at least 25½".
◆ Cut a strip of background 2½" by at least 25½".

Sew the two strips together. Press toward red. Cut off 2½" units (1C). Arrange and sew to create a Four Patch as shown previously.

1904

Alex Anderson; hand quilted by Kristina Volker
This quilt is 71" x 71" and contains twenty-five 12" 1904 stars.

Fabric Tips

When I think of using the jewel colors represented in this quilt, black traditionally comes to mind for the background fabric. Using white instead gives the quilt a bright, crisp look. When working with colors that are predominantly on one side of the color wheel, think of adding a touch of the color found directly across on the wheel. This adds spice. When my friend Kris Volker quilted this, she felt the border needed further embellishment, so perle cotton fringe was added to the cactus. Let your quilt talk to you. The direction it takes might surprise you!

Fabric Requirements

The following instructions give the total yardage needed to complete your quilt. (See General Instructions: Yardage, page 8.)

Purple/Pink Stars: 2¾ yards

Blue/Greens: ¾ yard

White Background: 3¼ yards

Orange Inner Border and Accent: ½ yard

Border and Accent Triangles: 2¼ yards

Backing: 4¼ yards

12" 1904

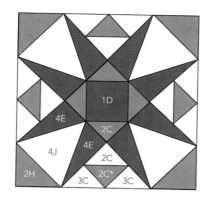

CUTTING

Traditional: use template patterns 1D, 4E, 2C, 2H, 4J, 3C.

The following numbers are for one 12" 1904 star. You will need twenty-five in all. (See General Instructions: Cutting, page 8.)

Star Body

- ◆ Cut one 3½" square (1D).
- ◆ Cut a strip 2⅞" by at least 23". Fold and press end to end, like sides together. Cut two rectangles 2⅞" x 5½". Then cut on the diagonal as shown (4E).

- ◆ Cut two 3" squares, then cut ◩ (2C).
- ◆ Cut two 3" squares of the accent fabric, then cut ◩ (2C*). (Cut from the length wise grain of fabric so the border does not have to be pieced.)
- ◆ Cut two 3⅞" squares, then cut ◩ (2H).

Background

- ◆ Cut a 5⅛" wide strip of fabric selvage to selvage.

From the end of the strip mark 5⅛" increments down the length of the strip. (Use this cutting technique when the background fabric is the same.)

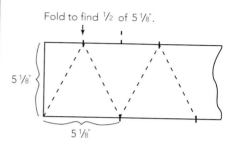

Fold in half to find the center of this first 5⅛" increment and mark on the opposite side. From this point, measure and mark 5⅛" increments down the length of the strip. (Save the extra for other stars.) Or use template pattern 4J.

- ◆ Cut two 3" squares, then cut ◩ (2C).
- ◆ Cut two 4¼" squares, then cut ◪ (3C).

(Keep these sets of triangles in the proper place. The outside edge of the block will then be on the straight of grain).

PIECING AND PRESSING

Follow the diagram below for piecing sequence. The ^ indicates which edge or point to line up (see All-Star Lineup, pages 8-9). The arrows indicate which way to press (see Pressing, page 10).

1. Sew center unit and press.

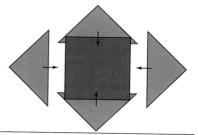

2. Sew star points and press.

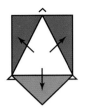

3. Sew side units and press.

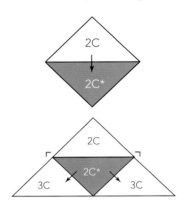

4. Sew all the units together and press. Note that this is a diagonal set.

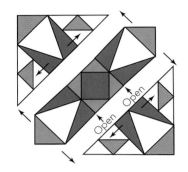

Borders

This quilt has mitered borders. Refer to a basic quiltmaking book for instructions on mitered borders. Feel free to use straight borders.

Inner Border
◆ Cut and piece four strips 1" x 64".

Outer Border
◆ Cut four strips 5½" x 76".

Setting

1. Arrange your blocks as shown.
2. Sew on the inner border.
3. Sew on the outer border. Good job! Your quilt is now ready to layer, baste, and quilt.

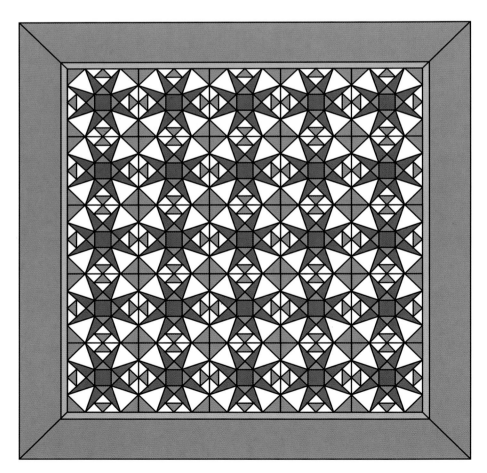

1904

Pieced and machine quilted by Alex Anderson

12" Shining Brighter

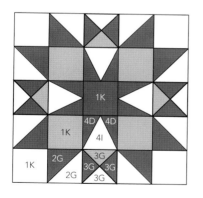

Traditional: use template patterns 1K, 4D, 2G, 3G, 4I.

Star Body

- Cut one 2⅞" square (1K).
- Cut one strip 1⅞" by at least 16". Fold and press end to end, like sides together. Cut two rectangles 1⅞" x 3⅝". Then cut on the diagonal as shown (4D).

- Cut four 3¼" squares, then cut ◲ (2G).
- Cut two 3⅝" squares, then cut ⊠ (3G).

Background

- Cut four 3¼" squares, then cut as shown. (This cut produces a lot of waste. If fabric conservation is important, please use template pattern 4I.)

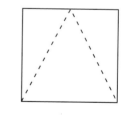

- Cut eight 2⅞" squares (1K). (Note how two different fabrics were used.)
- Cut four 3¼" squares, then cut ◲ (2G).
- Cut two 3⅝" squares, then cut ⊠ (3G). (Note how two different fabrics were used.)

PIECING AND PRESSING

Follow the diagram below for piecing sequence. The ^ indicates which edge or point to line up (see All-Star Lineup, pages 8-9). The arrows indicate which way to press (see Pressing, page 10).

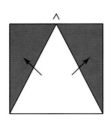

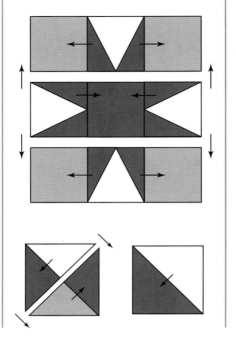

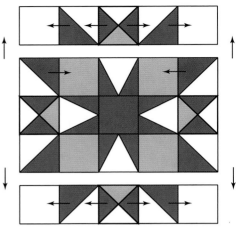

STARS

MADE OF DIAMONDS AND Y SEAMS

Continuous as the stars that shine
And twinkle on the Milky Way,
They stretched in never-ending line
Along the margin of a bay:
Ten thousand saw I, at a glance,
Tossing their head in a sprightly dance.

—William Wordsworth, 1850

Le Moyne Star

Alex Anderson; machine quilted by Susanne M. Rasmussen
This quilt is 71"x 71" and contains thirty-six 6" Le Moyne Stars.

Fabric Tips

I hit the jackpot when this focus fabric crossed my path. It had a multitude of colors that were extremely unusual put together in one print. I took the lead from the fabric and combined colors that might make a person feel uncomfortable. For example, check out the pink and orange! When selecting fabric for the star, it was important to keep the star tips of similar value; otherwise, the star would look unbalanced.

I love using many different background fabrics. Notice how this collection of background fabrics introduced white into the quilt. White always adds sparkle.

Fabric Requirements

The following instructions give the total yardage needed to complete your quilt. (See General Instructions: Yardage, page 8.)

Focus Fabric: 4 yards

Stars: 1 yard

Star Background and Geese Border: 2 yards

First Inner Border: ¼ yard

Backing: 4¼ yards

6" Le Moyne Star

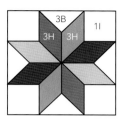

CUTTING

Traditional: use template patterns 3H, 3B, 1I.

The following numbers are for one 6" Le Moyne star. You will need thirty-six in all. (See General Instructions: Cutting, page 8.)

Star Body

◆ Cut one 1¾" strip selvage to selvage. Cut off the end at 45°. Keeping the ruler at 45° move the ruler over 1¾" and cut (3H). Repeat seven times on seven different strips of fabric. (Save the leftover strips for other blocks.)

Background

◆ Cut one 3¾" square, then cut ⊠ (3B).
◆ Cut four 2¼" squares (1I).

Mark a dot ¼" in from the corner of the triangles and squares on the wrong side of the fabric. This is your stop and start point that will create the Y seam.

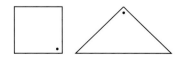

PIECING AND PRESSING

Follow the diagram below for piecing sequence. The ^ indicates which edge or point to line up (see All-Star Lineup, pages 8-9). The arrows indicate which way to press (see Pressing, page 10).

Piece the following units as shown. Sew in the direction the arrow indicates. Always stop and backstitch at the dot. Pin as needed (see Pinning, page 10). Only press when indicated. Use a colored thread that matches the star body.

1. Piece unit A. (This is called a Y seam.)

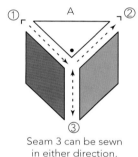

Seam 3 can be sewn in either direction.

2. Press.

Press Open

3. Piece a 2¼" square to unit A and press, creating unit B.

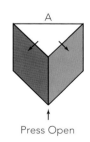

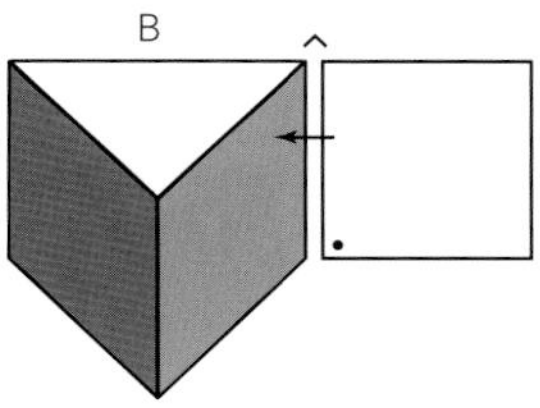

4. Piece two unit B's and press, creating unit C. (Pin so the center seams are aligned exactly.)

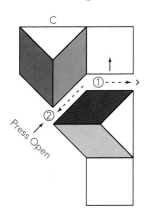

5. Piece two unit C's and press, creating unit D. (Pin so the center seams are aligned exactly.)

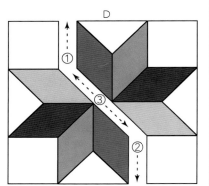

Press Center Seam Open

Border

Cut focus fabric inner border strips first so you won't have to piece the border. The border has eighty-eight 2" x 8" Double Flying Geese. Each unit is separated by a ¾" x 8" strip of focus fabric.

Geese

Traditional: use template patterns 3D, 2F, 2B.

◆ Cut forty-four 5¼" squares of background fabric, then cut ⊠ (3D).

Background (Focus Fabric)

◆ Cut twenty-two 5¼" squares, then cut ⊠ (3D).
◆ Cut eighty-eight 2⅞" squares, then cut ◹ (2F).
◆ Cut ninety-two rectangles 1¼" x 8½" (2B).

Piece and press as shown. (See All-Star Lineup, pages 8-9, for point positions.)

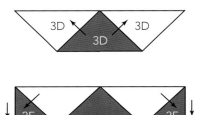

Sew twenty-two double geese units into one row, separating each unit with a 1¼" x 8½" strip. Each row will have a 1¼" x 8½" background strip on both ends.

Alternate Blocks (Focus Fabric)

Traditional: use template pattern 1G.

◆ Cut twenty-five 6½" squares (1G).

Side Quarter Triangles (Focus Fabric)

◆ Cut five 9¾" squares, then cut ⊠. (No template pattern given.)

Corner Triangles (Focus Fabric)

◆ Cut two 5⅛" squares, then cut ◺. (No template pattern given.)

First Inner Border

◆ Cut and piece two strips 1¼" x 51½".
◆ Cut and piece two strips 1¼" x 53".

Focus Fabric Inner Border

◆ Cut and piece two strips 1¾" x 53".
◆ Cut and piece two strips 1¾" x 55½".

Setting

1. Arrange your blocks as shown in diagram. Note that they are set on point.

2. Join the pieced blocks and the side and corner triangles in a diagonal set.

3. Sew on the first inner border, sides first, then top and bottom. Repeat for the second inner border.

4. Sew on the outer Double Flying Geese border. Note how the corner geese strips have been rotated to create a continuous, intertwining clockwise motion. "Thumbs up" to the Y seam; it can be used in so many places!

With a little organization and practice, you should be able to make these stars in record time. I can now assemble one star in fifteen minutes. No kidding. Just practice; I know you can do it!

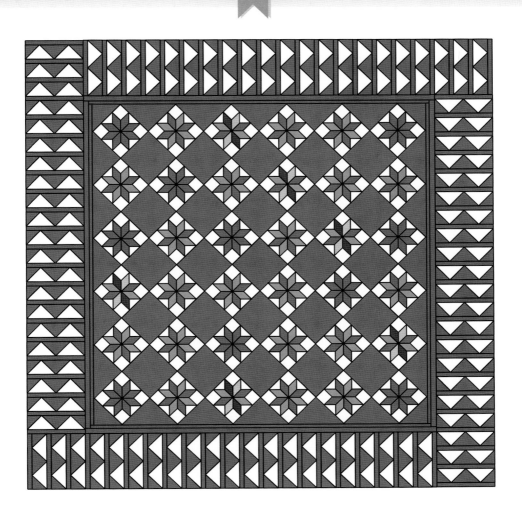

Le Moyne Bonus Numbers

If you have fallen in love with making the Le Moyne as I have, you might enjoy piecing this little star in other sizes. The given numbers are the cutting numbers, and have the seam allowances included. (No template patterns given.)

Finished Size of Block	Diamonds	Squares	Quarter-Square Triangles
4"	1⅜"	1¾"	2⅞"
5"	1½"	2"	3¼"
6"	1¾"	2¼"	3¾"
7"	2"	2⅝"	4⅜"
8"	2⅛"	2⅞"	4½"
9"	2⅜"	3⅛"	5"
10"	2⅝"	3½"	5⅜"
11"	2¾"	3¾"	5⅞"
12"	3"	4"	6¼"

Memory

Alex Anderson; machine quilted by Susanne M. Rasmussen
This quilt is 57" x 57" and contains sixteen 12" Memory stars.

Fabric Tips

Purple is not one of the first colors I would choose to work with. However, I met the challenge by starting with a purple and green focus fabric (used in the inner border and repeated in each of the stars). Other fabrics were then used to coordinate with this print. Two background fabrics were used and arranged in a diagonal manner. The diagonal arrangement of the background fabric was then extended into the border. Note how the half-square triangles move around the border in different three color sets. These little tricks help create order in this quilt.

Fabric Requirements

The following instructions give the total yardage needed to complete your quilt. (See General Instructions: Yardage, page 8.)

Focus Fabric: 1⅔ yards
Purple: ¾ yard
Pink: ¾ yard
Green: 1 yard
Background: 2 yards
Backing: 3⅓ yards

12" Memory

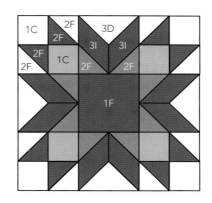
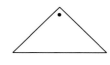

CUTTING

Traditional: use template patterns 1F, 2F, 1C, 3I, 3D.

The following numbers are for one 12" Memory star. You will need sixteen in all. (See General Instructions: Cutting, page 8.)

I recommend you cut the inner border from the length of your focus fabric first so you won't have to piece it later. Be generous in the length of the cut; you can trim it to the exact size later.

Star Body

◆ Cut one 4½" square (1F).
◆ Cut a total of eight 2⅞" squares (four of each fabric), then cut ◻ (2F).
◆ Cut four 2½" squares (1C).
◆ Cut one 2" strip selvage to selvage. Fold and press end to end, like sides together. Cut off the end at 45°. Keeping the ruler at 45°, move the ruler over 2½" and cut (3I). Repeat three times.

Background

◆ Cut four 2½" squares (1C).
◆ Cut four 2⅞" squares, then cut ◻ (2F).
◆ Cut one 5¼" square, then cut ⊠ (3D).

Mark a dot ¼" in from the corner on the wrong side of the fabric on triangle 3D. This is your stop and start point that will create the Y seam.

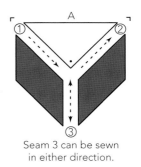

PIECING AND PRESSING

Follow the diagram below for piecing sequence. The ^ indicates which edge or point to line up (see All-Star Lineup, pages 8-9). Piece the following units as shown. Pin as needed (see Pinning, page 10). The arrows indicate which way to press (see Pressing, page 10). Only press when indicated.

1. Piece unit A. (This is called a Y seam.) Sew in the direction the arrow indicates. Stop and backstitch at the dot.

Seam 3 can be sewn in either direction.

2. Press.

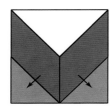

Press Open

3. Sew side triangles onto this unit.

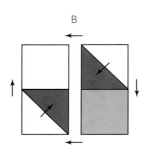

4. Piece and press unit B.

B

5. Assemble rows one, two, and three.

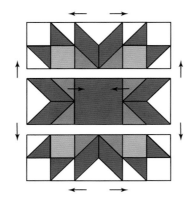

Inner Border (Focus Fabric)

◆ Cut two strips 2" x 48½".
◆ Cut two strips 2" x 51½".

Outer Border

The border is made up of one hundred thirty-six 3" half-square triangles pieced from the various fabrics used in this quilt.

Traditional: use template patterns 2H, 1D.

◆ Cut thirty-four 3⅞" squares of colored prints, then cut ◻ (2H).
◆ Cut thirty-four 3⅞" squares of the two background fabrics, then cut ◻ (2H).
◆ Cut four 3½" squares for corner blocks (1D).

Piece the half-square triangles together, press toward dark, and arrange as shown. You will need seventeen units for each side. Remember to add a corner square on both ends of the top and bottom borders. Note how the triangles have changed direction at random. This is an unusual way to handle turning the corners. Before sewing your triangles into rows, try arranging them in a different order. You might be pleasantly surprised with the results.

Setting

1. Arrange your blocks as shown in diagram.
2. Join your blocks in a straight set.
3. Sew on the inner border, sides first, then top and bottom.
4. Sew on the pieced outer border, sides first, then top and bottom.

You did it! Your quilt is now ready to layer, baste, and quilt.

Split Le Moyne Star

Alex Anderson; machine quilted by Susanne M. Rasmussen
This quilt is 67" x 67" and contains thirteen 12" Split Le Moyne Stars.

Fabric Tips

If your background is light, use a dark and medium fabric for the star body. Fabrics with stripes or a directional pattern are especially wonderful for the Split Le Moyne. The diamond shape has all bias edges, so be wary of fabric without a lot of body. My recommendation is to first try your hand with a regular Le Moyne star before you approach this block.

Fabric Requirements

The following instructions give the total yardage needed to complete your quilt. (See General Instructions: Yardage, page 8.)

Star Body
Medium: 1¼ yards
Dark: 1¼ yards
Star Background: 1½ yards
Side and Corner Triangles
Background: 1 yard
First Inner Border: ⅓ yard
Second Inner Border: ⅓ yard
Border: 2 yards
Backing: 4 yards

12" Split Le Moyne Star

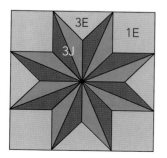

CUTTING

The following numbers are for one 12" Split Le Moyne star. You will need thirteen in all (see General Instructions: Cutting, page 8.)

Star Body

1. Use a colored thread that matches the star body.
2. Trace and cut template 3J out of see-through template plastic material. Draw a line down the center of the template.

3. Cut one strip of fabric from both star fabrics selvage to selvage, using your template as a guide. The width of the strip is not an exact measurement. For this 12" block it will be about 3½".

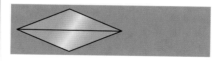

4. Sew the two strips together.
5. Press to set the seam, then press the seam open.
6. Heavily spray starch the sewn strips of fabric.

CUTTING

1. Place the template plastic on the pieced strip with the drawn line lined up on the open seam. Mark around the template with

a sharp pencil or permanent pen. Cut shapes along inside of marked lines.

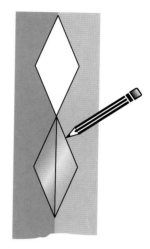

Caution: Do not cut all the way to the edge of the fabric.
You will get five diamonds from the width of the fabric. Sew the two uncut sides of the leftover fabric together.

2. Press the seam open.
3. Cut three more diamonds from this strip.

Background

Traditional: use template patterns 3E, 1E.

- ◆ Cut one 6¼" square, then cut ⊠ (3E).
- ◆ Cut four 4" squares (1E).

Mark a dot ¼" in from the corner on the wrong side of the fabric on the triangles and squares as shown.

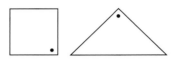

PIECING AND PRESSING

Follow the diagram below for piecing sequence. The ^ indicates which edge or point to line up (see All-Star Lineup, pages 8-9). The arrows indicate which way to press (see Pressing, page 10).

Piece the following units as shown. Sew in the direction the arrow indicates. Backstitch at the dot. Pin as needed (see Pinning, page 10). If at any time the interior split is not perfectly matched up, carefully pick out stitches, repin and sew. When opening and pressing seams, be extremely careful not to stretch the bias edges. If you ignore this warning, your star will end up looking like a party hat or some other piece of clothing that fits a body part! Take your time and good luck.

1. Piece unit A. (This is called a Y seam.)

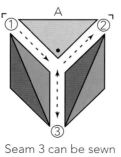

Seam 3 can be sewn in either direction.

2. Press.

Press Open

3. Piece unit B and press toward square.

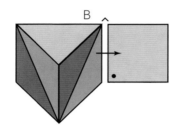

4. Piece unit C and only press open seam 2.

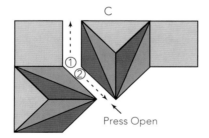

Press Open

5. Piece unit D. To ensure a flat star, make sure all seams are pressed as indicated.

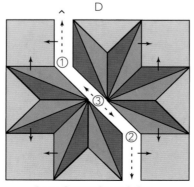

Press Center Seam 3 Open

First Inner Border

- ◆ Cut and piece two strips 1½" x 51½".
- ◆ Cut and piece two strips 1½" x 53½".

Second Inner Border

- ◆ Cut and piece two strips 1½" x 53½".
- ◆ Cut and piece two strips 1½" x 55½".

Outer Border

- ◆ Cut two strips 6½" x 55½".
- ◆ Cut two strips 6½" x 67½".

Side Quarter-Square Triangles

- ◆ Cut two 18¼" squares, then cut ⊠. (No template pattern given.)

Corner Triangles

- ◆ Cut two 9⅜" squares, then cut ◺. (No template pattern given.)

Setting

1. Lay out your blocks as shown in diagram. Note that they are set on point.

2. Join the pieced blocks and the side and corner triangles in a diagonal set.

3. Sew on the first inner border, then the second inner border, sides first, then top and bottom.

4. Sew on the outer floral border, top and bottom first, then sides.

Congratulations. Once you've mastered this star, you can piece anything. Only the sky is your limit!

Wyoming Valley Star

Pieced and machine quilted by Alex Anderson

12" Wyoming Valley Star

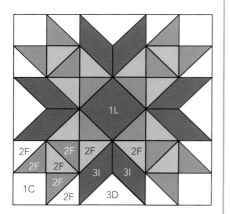

Traditional: use template patterns 1L, 2F, 3I, 1C.

Star Body

◆ Cut one 3⅜" square (1L).
◆ Cut a total of fourteen 2⅞" squares, using as many different fabrics as desired, then cut ◳ (2F).

◆ Cut one 2" strip selvage to selvage. Fold and press end to end, like sides together. Cut off the end at 45°. Keeping the ruler at 45°, move the ruler over 2½" and cut (3I). Repeat three times.

Background

◆ Cut four 2½" squares (1C).
◆ Cut four 2⅞" squares, then cut ◳ (2F).
◆ Cut one 5¼" square, then cut ⊠ (3D).

PIECING AND PRESSING

Follow the diagram below for piecing sequence. The arrows indicate which way to press (see Pressing, page 10.)

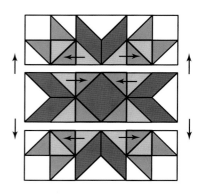

Press Open

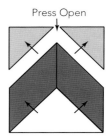

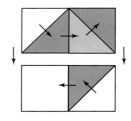

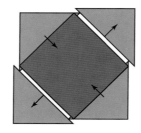

A STELLAR ENDING

Setting

As your stars begin to develop, you will need to start thinking about the size and setting of your quilt. This process should occur when the quilt is about sixty percent finished. The quilt can be as small as a table runner or as large as a circus tent. The choice is yours. It is at this point you need to pay attention to what is happening colorwise with the different blocks.

We have been working with six-inch and twelve-inch stars. They will fit quite easily into over a million different sets; you just need a plan. Some people feel comfortable charting a setting on graph paper; others, like myself, prefer putting the blocks up on the design wall, using an imaginary grid and spacing the two sized blocks out in irregular patterns. Think of the quilt top as a jigsaw puzzle. Until you become familiar with this system, consider setting the irregular blocks in rows. This will help you avoid piecing problems. Here are two examples of simple sets.

twenty-eight 6" blocks and nine 12" blocks

Place the star blocks you have made so far into the desired grid. Look carefully and assess what is happening as you complete the rest of your blocks. Here are some tips to keep in mind as you arrange and play with your blocks.

1. If any fabric jumps out at you, it's time to repeat it. Just as in flower arranging, the number of fabrics should be odd. The 6" Sawtooth Stars come in handy for this. It is also OK to repeat the fabric in just a star tip. Make sure the eye-catching color is placed across the entire quilt top, not just in one corner or half. You want the eye to travel across the entire surface when looking at the quilt.

2. If all the background fabrics are primarily light, you might find your quilt is looking "flat." To add some punch, consider introducing some dark background/light stars to the mix. Once again, the 6" stars really come in handy at times like this.

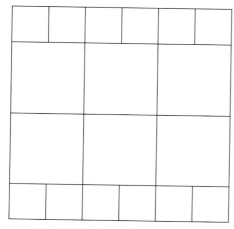

twelve 6" blocks and six 12" blocks

85

3. Consider putting high-contrast blocks in each of the corners. This will help hold the quilt together.

4. Consider introducing other blocks or components into the quilt using shapes from the star blocks. Take, for example, the half-square triangle we have used so many times. From this simple shape you can get Flying Geese, Pinwheels, Squares on Point, Zigzags, and many other shapes. Just let your imagination take over. The shapes can provide a place for the eye to rest or add an interesting design element to the quilt (see Leslie Skibo's quilt, page 29). Just remember to keep the shapes in sizes that are multiples of twelve inches. I like to work with half-square triangles that are two inches when finished.

5. Determine whether your quilt design would be enhanced by sashing (see Melanie Bobbitt's and Blanche Young's quilts, pages 32 and 35, respectively). Sometimes a sashing appears to be an afterthought or simply a way to make the quilt larger. Consider other options, e.g., a pieced sashing with appropriate corner posts to complement the overall design.

6. Consider adding appliqué to your pieced quilt. Sometimes appliqué adds the perfect finishing touch. In some cases appliqué is essential to the piece (see Emma Allebes, Rosemary Houser, and Cindy Slyker's quilt, pages 30, 36, and 28, respectively).

Borders

Inner Border

There is no hard and fast rule about whether to use an inner border or not. What you need to consider is whether the quilt needs a resting place before the border is attached. If it does, keep the inner border to one inch finished. Then the math work will not be thrown off.

If one fabric is great, why not use two, three, or four? (See Maureen Atteberry's quilt, page 28.) Remember, more is better! If you are using a stripe, consider cutting and rotating segments to add extra interest. It is always a good idea to take the obvious method and add a twist. This is when freedom and creativity start to take form.

Different borders

Outer Borders

Think about the amount of time you want to further invest in your quilt. Personally, I like pieced borders; however, there are times when a non-pieced border is appropriate. If you used a focus fabric in the quilt, adding it to the border can often add the glorious finishing touch. In addition, consider using two fabrics for the border, instead of one. This can create an interesting effect without too much effort. (See Maureen Atteberry's quilt, page 28.)

As I mentioned above, pieced borders top my list. When I think about what to use for the pieced border, I look first to the blocks that make up the quilt. I study them carefully and assess which shapes are used over and over. More than likely with a star quilt, it will be triangles. Then I consider other blocks or pieced units made up of those shapes (see the Setting section, step 4 on page 85). Remember to keep the units in two-inch finished increments so the math work will not be a problem. (See Patty Scott-Baier's quilt, page 30.)

A border can change as it works its way around the quilt. There is no reason you can't combine a non-pieced section on one side of the quilt with a pieced section on the other side. (See Leslie Ison's and Melanie Bobbitt's quilts, pages 33 and 32, respectively.) As you approach a design situation, think of several alternate possibilities. Reward the viewer who stops to look at your quilt. If you keep the attitude of "How can I change the look of the quilt," the design process will remain fresh and alive throughout the entire process.

Backing

The back of a quilt can be just as interesting as the front. Pieced quilt backs that incorporate several fabrics from the front bring interesting results. The back is also an excellent place to use up stars that just didn't "cut the mustard" for the front of the quilt. If you have focus fabric left over, the back is a perfect place to use it up. Feel free to piece it with a few companion pieces. There is no rule that says the back of a quilt needs to be all of the same fabric, and it's fun to surprise people who ask the white-glove lady to turn the quilt over to see the back.

I can add only two cautions when deciding on which fabric to use on the back.

1. Use 100% cottons purchased from your quilting store. Never use a sheet or decorator fabric because they have a high thread count and are difficult to quilt through. I often bring my quilting needle and take a few passes through a fabric before purchasing it. If the fabric seems to grab or react to the needle in a stubborn way, I will pass it by to find another piece in which the needle glides through nicely. If you are machine quilting, this is not an issue.

2. If your quilt top is light in color, make sure the backing is also light. Choosing a dark backing may dull the brightness of your quilt by showing through the batting and top.

Remember to sign and date your quilt (with a permanent ink pen)! This will add value to it for future generations.

Quilting

As a self-admitted quilting snob, I have three simple philosophies that apply to quilting.

- ◆ More is better.
- ◆ Treat the pieced surface as one.
- ◆ Have an equal amount of quilting across the entire surface.

Whether you are hand or machine quilting, give due consideration to the design and workmanship.

Star quilts have a lot of activity in them, so usually a simple quilted grid pattern will suffice. If you have a heavily pieced surface with many exciting fabric combinations, an intricate quilting design will not show; however, the total amount of quilting will!

Look at your pieced top for several days before you determine how to quilt it. Here are a few guidelines I always keep in mind when determining the approach I want to take.

1. We spend so much time piecing our tops; when it comes time to quilt, we think we are on the home stretch. But the amount of quilting you put into your quilt should never be short-changed or come as an afterthought. Whether you are an avid hand quilter or a converted machine quilter, you need to have adequate quilting on your pieced surface. This alone can make or break the quilt.

2. I always approach the pieced top as one unit, never as a series of individual blocks. Many people tend to quilt ¼" in around the seams.

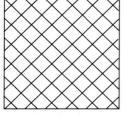
Crosshatch

Double Crosshatch

Zigzag

Mixed Diagonals

Soft Curves

This is how we direct beginners so they don't get bogged down in the process of picking up the needle to begin to quilt. Although this seems to be the simplest way to get started, I find it unsatisfactory because it pushes all the seam allowances up in your face. Even the simplest grid over the entire surface will provide charming results. You might want to try your hand at a ¾" repeated soft wave that covers the surface of the quilt, or a combination of both. By using an overall pattern, the blocks become less disjointed and unite as one. Here are some basic grid ideas that will get you started.

3. Along with a good amount of quilting, fill the surface with an equal amount of quilting. If you are using motifs, make sure they fill the space. This will keep areas from sagging.

4. If you are hand quilting, consider using a low-loft poly batt for ease of the stitch. If you are machine quilting, use a 100% cotton batt. An excellent batt that works well in both situations is Hobbs Heirloom®.

5. Keeping these basic rules in mind, I look to quilts of the past for inspiration and design ideas.

Binding

Last, but not least, comes the binding. Even though picking the fabric for your binding may seem like a non-decision, here is the last place you can again sew your creative spirit into the quilt. If you look carefully at all the quilts presented, you will see the bindings are pieced from many fabrics. I like this technique because it is a great way to introduce a variety of fabrics into my quilt. This is also an excellent place to frame and put your signature on the quilt.

All the tips discussed in this book can be incorporated when making a quilt composed of traditional blocks. These fabric and design guidelines have stood the test of time. I have used these rules with Baskets, Houses, the Maple Leaf, and many other traditional blocks. But remember, *rules were made to be broken*. Keep your instincts in tune and deviate when necessary.

Expose yourself to other people's work through magazines, books, quilt shows, and classes. Look at what other quilters have made and consider all the elements used in creating their quilts. Incorporate what is pleasing from theirs into your next quilt. We are in the midst of a quilting renaissance, and are so fortunate to have each other to learn from. Take advantage of it! It is only your imagination that will limit you. My wish for you is to create, have fun, and grow through the wonderful world of star making!

Escape at Bedtime

The lights from the parlor and kitchen shone out
Through the blinds and the windows and bars;
And high over head and moving about,
There were thousands and millions of stars.
There ne'er were such thousands of leaves on a tree,
Nor of people in church or the park,
As the crowds of the stars that looked down upon me,
And that glittered and winked in the park.

The Dog, and the Plough, and the Hunter, and all,
And the star of the sailor, and Mars,
These shone in the sky, and the pail by the wall
Would be half full of water and stars.
They saw me at last, and they chased me with cries,
And soon they packed me into bed;
But the glory kept shining and bright in my eyes,
And the stars going round in my head.

—Robert Louis Stevenson, 1894

Template Patterns
¼" seam allowance included

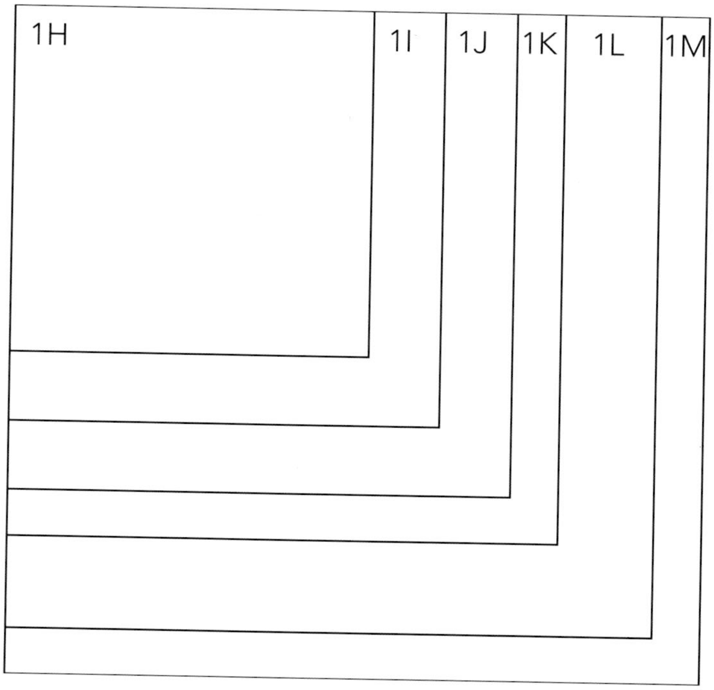

1H

1I

1J

1K

1L

1M

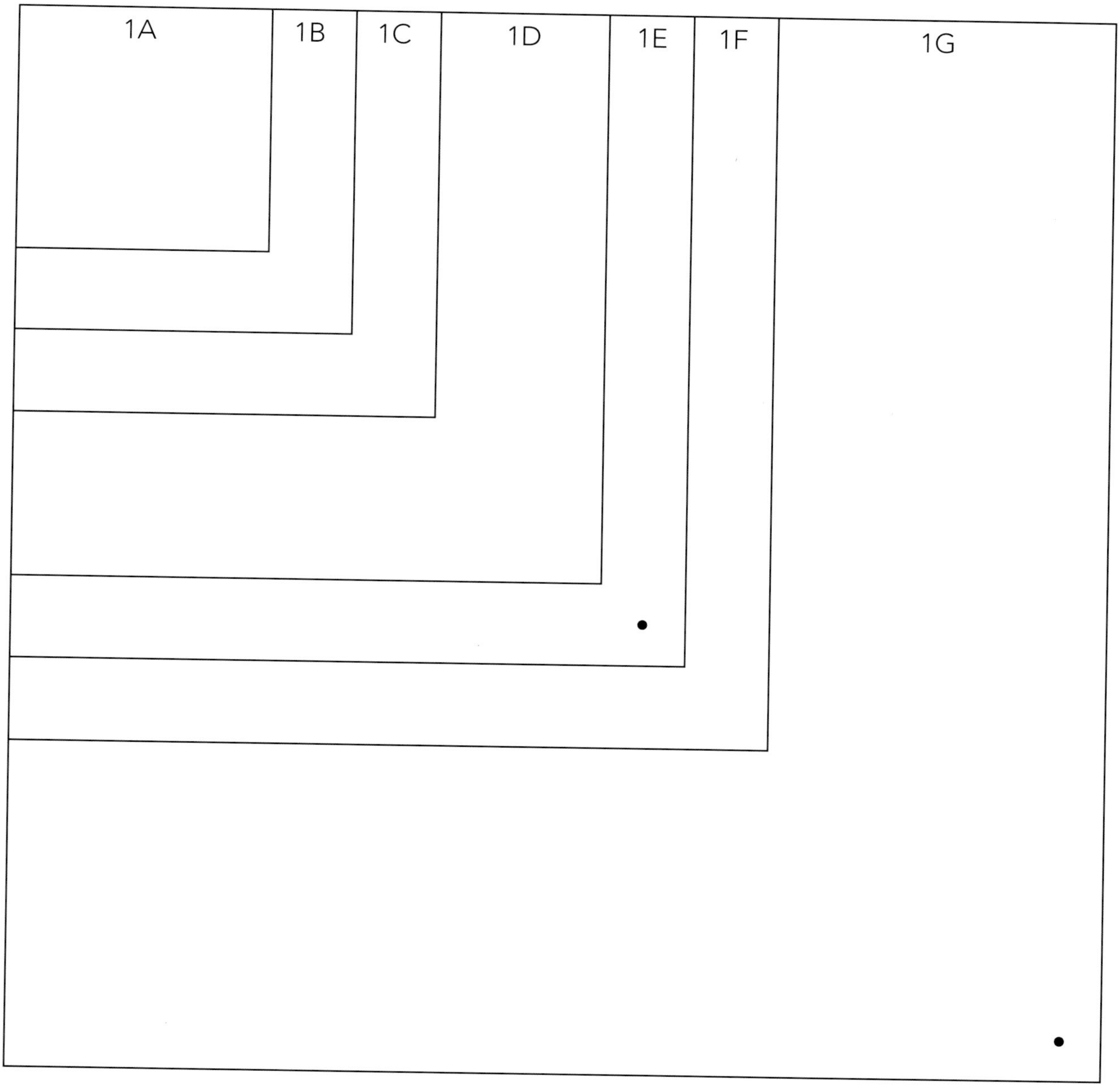

1A

1B

1C

1D

1E

1F

1G

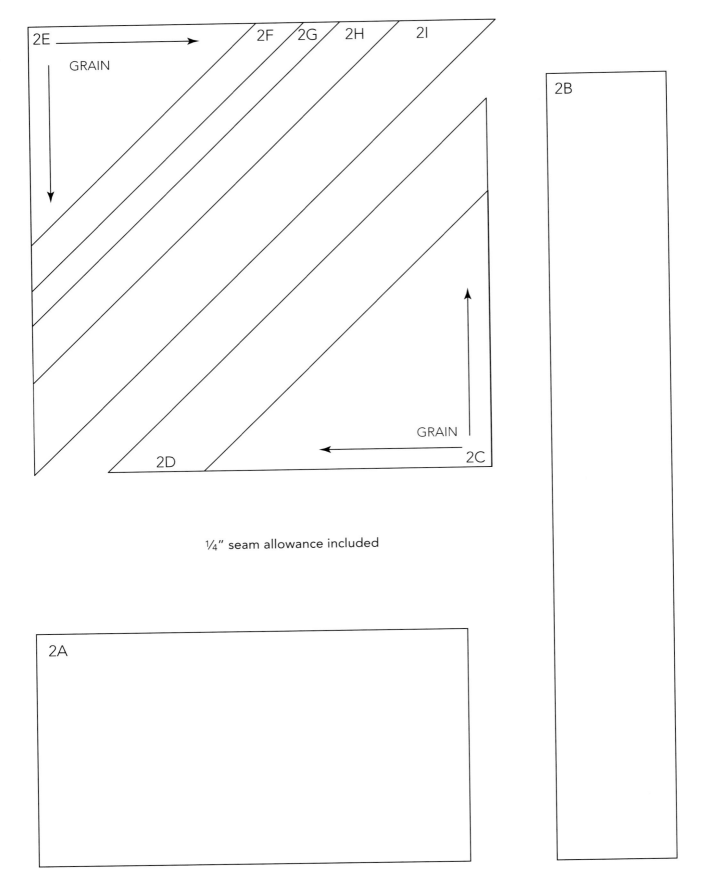

¼" seam allowance included

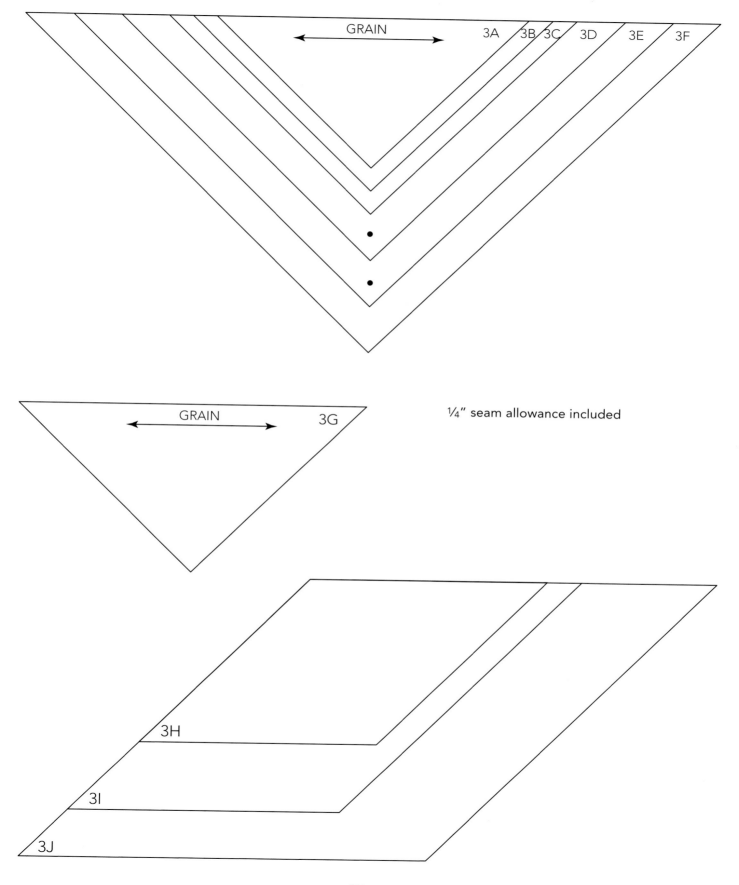

GRAIN

3A 3B 3C 3D 3E 3F

GRAIN 3G

¼" seam allowance included

3H

3I

3J

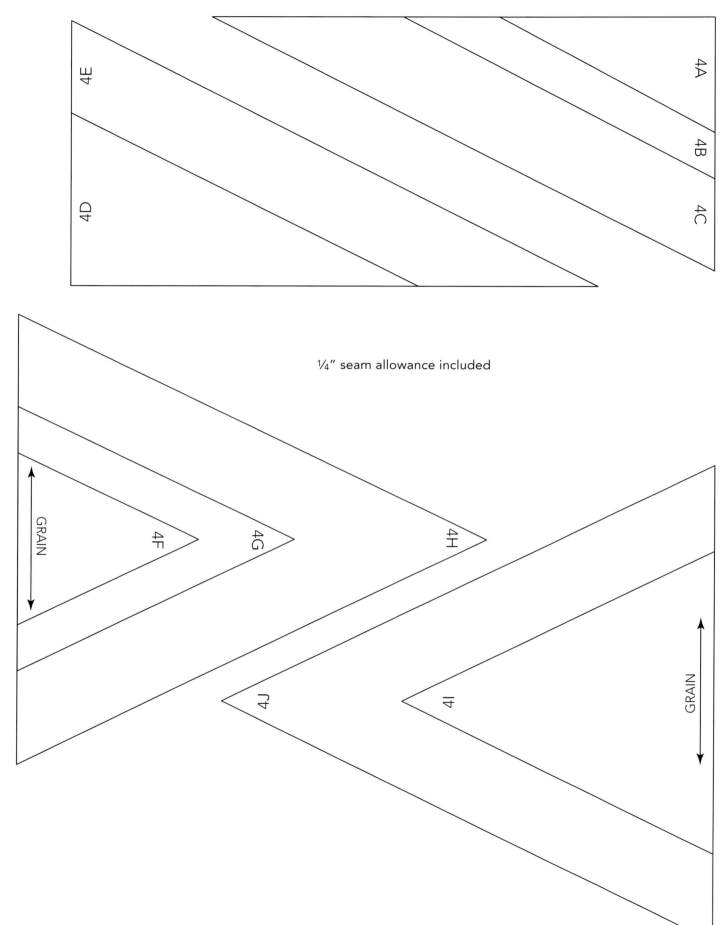

4A

4B

4C

4E

4D

¼" seam allowance included

GRAIN

4F

4G

4H

4J

4I

GRAIN

Simply Stars provides a terrific format for a four-week class geared to quilters with one year or more of quilting experience. Stars challenge students with unusual piecing situations, and the sampler format allows quilters to create freely with unusual fabric combinations. I like to encourage quilters to work with fabric sets they are unfamiliar with; it's wonderful to see the development and diversity of each class.

Supplies

- Text: *Simply Stars: Quilts that Sparkle* by Alex Anderson (C&T Publishing)
- Fabric: To start, twelve ¼ yard cuts of fabric of coordinated fabric (additional fabric will be added after the first class)
- Sewing machine in working order, iron, extension cord
- Sewing notions
- Rotary cutter and mat (a mat with a grid works best)
- 6" x 12" Omnigrid® ruler
- Spray starch or sizing
- Pellon® Fleece to hang your stars on

Class format:

Four three-hour classes

CLASS ONE

Introductions: Teacher shares overview of class format.

Stars Made of Squares and Triangles

Discussion:
1. Talk about the different ideas of choosing a fabric set.
2. Magic (cutting) numbers that relate to squares and triangles.
3. Lining up the odd shapes as shown in the All-Star Lineup.

Demonstration:
4. Piece a 6" Sawtooth Star.
While piecing, verbally cover the information discussed in Points, Pinning, and Pressing.

Classwork:
5. Help students with fabric choices.
6. Students start piecing Sawtooth Star in class.

Homework: Work on stars in Squares and Triangles unit.

CLASS TWO

Stars Made of an Isosceles Triangle in a Square

Discussion:
1. Students display work on walls and discuss any problems or discoveries.
2. Magic (cutting) numbers that relate to the isosceles triangle in a square.
3. Lining up the odd shapes as shown in the All-Star Lineup.

Demonstration:
4. Piece a 12" 54/40 or Fight Star.

Classwork:
5. Students start piecing a 54/40 or Fight Star in class.

Homework: Work on stars in isosceles triangles in a square unit.

CLASS THREE

Stars Made with a 45° Cut and Y seam

Discussion:
1. Students display work on walls and discuss any problems or discoveries.
2. Magic (cutting) numbers that relate to 45° diamonds.

Demonstration:
3. Cut the star out, demonstrating how to use a rotary ruler with the 45° angle successfully .
4. Piece a 12" Le Moyne.

Classwork:
5. Students start cutting and piecing a 12" Le Moyne Star in class.

Homework: Work on stars in 45°, Y seam unit.

CLASS FOUR

Discussion:
1. Students display work on walls and discuss any problems or discoveries.
2. Discuss layout unit.
3. Discuss quilting and finishing.
4. Critique with class input on how to finish each student's quilt.
5. Piece a 12" Split Le Moyne.

Classwork:
6. Students start cutting and piecing a 12" split Le Moyne Star in class.

Homework: Finish quilt!

Star Gallery Quilts

Contributing Quiltmakers

ABOUT THE AUTHOR

Alex Anderson's love affair with quiltmaking began in 1978, when she completed her Grandmother's Flower Garden quilt as part of her work toward a degree in art at San Francisco State University. Her study of graphic design in fiber inspired in her a deep respect and admiration for Amish quilts. With their strong visual impact and sensitive intricacy of quilting design, they became the springboard for Alex's quiltmaking. Over the years her central focus has rested upon understanding fabric relationships, and an intense appreciation of traditional quilting surface design and star quilts.

For almost two decades Alex's quilts have been displayed in one-woman shows and have won prizes in group shows. She has lectured to numerous guilds, taught frequently at leading conferences, offered classes at several quilt shops, and currently hosts Home and Garden Television's quilt show *Simply Quilts*. Alex's works have been seen widely in a number of books by Diana McClun, Laura Nownes, Margaret Peters, Mary Coyne Penders, and Charlotte Warr Andersen. Her quilts have been shown in magazines, including several articles specifically about her works. She also worked with her father to develop his company, Sladky Quilt Frames. Her first book, *Quilts for Fabric Lovers*, which celebrates creative use of fabric, was published by C&T Publishing in the fall of 1994.

Alex lives in Northern California, with her husband, two children, two cats, one dog and its pet squirrel, one fish, and the challenges of step-aerobics and suburban life.

OTHER FINE BOOKS FROM C&T PUBLISHING:

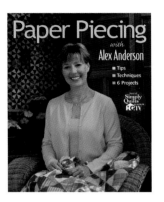

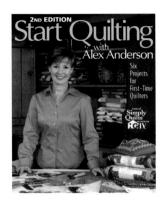

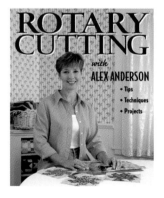

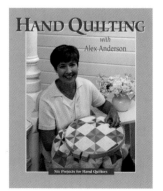

For more information write for a free catalog:
C&T Publishing, Inc.
P.O. Box 1456
Lafayette, CA 94549
(800) 284-1114
e-mail: ctinfo@ctpub.com
website: www.ctpub.com

For quilting supplies:
Cotton Patch Mail Order
3405 Hall Lane, Dept. CTB
Lafayette, CA 94549
(800) 835-4418
(925) 283-7883
e-mail: quiltusa@yahoo.com
website: www.quiltusa.com